Also by the Author

How School Administrators Make Things Happen, E. Howard and
E. Brainard

School Discipline Desk Book

Eugene R. Howard

Parker Publishing Company, Inc.

West Nyack, New York

© 1978, *by*

PARKER PUBLISHING COMPANY, INC.

West Nyack, N.Y.

Library of Congress Cataloging in Publication Data

Howard, Eugene R
    School discipline desk book.

    Bibliography: p.
    Includes index.
    1. School discipline. I. Title.
LB3012.H68   371.5   77-11921
ISBN 0-13-793000-3

Printed in the United States of America

To my wife, Virginia, who
personifies many of the ideals
to which this book is dedicated.

How This Book Can Help You
Improve Discipline in Your
Elementary or Secondary School

It is, perhaps, not a popular idea that the number and severity of our discipline problems could be reduced by modifying the nature of schools. It is simpler and more comfortable to blame many of the problems on such causes as lack of parental guidance, injustice in our society, the declining influence of churches, the dehumanizing influence of poverty, or the increase in violence portrayed in the public media. It is true that many of the causes of discipline problems lie within the nature of our society as well as within the nature of our schools. It is also true that we administrators and teachers can do little to reform society. *We can do a lot,* however, to improve schools.

Chapters 1 and 8 are success stories, describing in detail how one high school staff and one elementary school staff succeeded in drastically reducing discipline problems by applying some of the ideas suggested in this book. Through these chapters you will meet two dedicated and dynamic principals, William Maynard of the Cleveland High School in Seattle and Jo Ann Shaheen of the Blauvelt Elementary School in Cottage Lane,[1] New York. Both of these principals, by involving their pupils and staff in a variety of morale-building activities, succeeded in reducing the number of referrals to the office, reducing attendance problems, reducing disrespect, conflict and violence, and improving pupil achievement and morale. They are living proof that the ideas proposed in this book will work.

Other success stories are also reported. In Chapters 2 through 7, promising activities from nearly a hundred schools are described.

---

[1] A part of the South Orangetown Central School District.

Each idea presented for your consideration has been successfully implemented in several schools in various parts of the country. Most of the ideas can be implemented at either the elementary or secondary level.

You will notice that Chapters 2, 3, and 4 are devoted to three major approaches to "Shaping up a School"—that is, establishing a stable, orderly environment for learning and for further school improvement. Chapter 2 suggests fifty ideas which you might include in a plan to reduce crime and violence in your school. There are, for example, seventeen ideas for improving building security and nine suggestions for improving pupil behavior in the cafeteria.

Chapter 3 provides suggestions for improving the management of discipline and attendance problems. Included here are several ideas for managing such persistent problems as smoking and poor attendance. A final section of this chapter provides essential information for administrators so that they can manage discipline problems legally. "Keeping it legal" is becoming increasingly complex, as new definitions of due process and student rights are handed down periodically by the courts, legislatures, and the Congress.

Chapter 4 suggests ten ways administrators can help teachers improve discipline. One instrument, reproduced in its entirety in the Appendix C, enables a teacher to diagnose his own behavior in the classroom. Using the results of this diagnosis, the teacher can take appropriate action to reduce the number of discipline problems in his class.

Chapters 2, 3 and 4, then, provide immediate assistance to the administrator and teacher who want to manage day-to-day discipline problems efficiently, fairly, and legally. These chapters are designed to provide you and your colleagues with practical, easily implemented suggestions for dealing with the *symptoms* of discipline problems.

The next three chapters are concerned with *causes.*

Extensive evidence shows that the primary causes of discipline problems are deeply rooted in the nature of the school itself. Therefore, when school leaders decide to reduce the causes of the problems, they need to seek practical ways to modify the institution.

A number of schools, for example, are operated in such a way that it is inevitable some pupils will see themselves as failures by the age of ten. Schools, to some extent, create losers.

Chapter 5 is based on the assumption that the losers in the game of schooling will eventually turn against the school. The school, then, should be organized in such a way that harmful competition is reduced or eliminated so that as many pupils as possible feel that they are succeeding. Learning should be a win-win, not a win-lose process. Chapter 5 offers seven major suggestions for creating a win-win school.

Discipline problems are also caused by limitations of the extra-curricular programs (Chapter 6) and of the curriculum (Chapter 7). A wide variety of suggestions and instruments is offered for making the extracurriculum and the curriculum more responsive to student needs. The final section of Chapter 7 provides a variety of suggestions for implementing values education instruction in your school. The assumption underlying this section is that pupils' behavior is, to a large extent, a function of their beliefs and values. A number of promising curricula are now available which can positively affect pupil behavior by helping pupils adopt more mature systems of values and beliefs.

The bibliography, found in a special section following Chapter 8, is written in such a way that you and other leaders in your school can easily order materials to stock a professional library on improving discipline. The bibliography is more than just a documentation of sources; it is also a tool which can be used to provide valuable information to planning groups and task forces.

To improve discipline we advocate neither permissiveness nor a "get tough" policy. We suggest instead that the school must be managed efficiently and fairly in such a way that everyone's rights are respected. Substantial school improvement can take place only within an orderly environment.

Much has been written recently about the rights of those students, usually few in number, who present teachers and administrators with the majority of their discipline problems. We agree that these rights must be recognized.

We must also recognize, however, that students who are *not* discipline problems have rights. They have a right to go to a school where they will be free from fear; they have a right to an orderly positive learning environment.

This book will help you and your colleagues achieve and maintain such an environment.

E.R.H.

Acknowledgements

People from all over the country have contributed information for this book. I'am grateful to them for their willingness to share their ideas with others. I am especially grateful to five individuals who made substantial contributions of their time and expertise. These individuals are:

- Dr. Arlyn Gunderman, Principal, Reed Elementary School, St. Paul, Minnesota, who provided information used in several chapters.

- Dr. William Howard, formerly Superintendent, Reorganized School District #5, Kansas City, Missouri, who provided extensive information for Chapter 7.

- Dr. Larry Palmatier and Dr. Jon Davis, Professors of Education, University of Utah, Salt Lake City, who authored the parts of Chapter 7 and the Appendix dealing with values education.

- Dr. Jo Ann Shaheen, Principal, Blauvelt Elementary School, South Orangetown Central School District, New York, who sent me tapes and materials describing the Blauvelt program (see Chapter 8).

- Dr. William Maynard, Principal, Cleveland High School, Seattle, Washington, who provided the information for Chapter 1.

I am also grateful to CADRE (Collegial Associates for the Development and Renewal of Educators), a small, national professional organization dedicated to humanizing the organizational climate of schools. Many of the ideas for this book were volunteered by my colleagues in that organization.

Eugene R. Howard

Table of Contents

7. Improving Student Morale by Modifying the Curriculum . . . 142

8. Achieving More Effective Discipline by Improving Self Esteem— A Snapshot of What's Happening in Cottage Lane, New York 167

Getting It Together in
An Urban High School –
A Snapshot of
Cleveland High School in Seattle

1

THE PROBLEM

Five years ago Cleveland High School was plagued with all of the problems usually associated with high schools which serve low-income neighborhoods. The symptoms:

- A high dropout rate. Forty percent of the students who entered the 10th grade dropped out before graduation.

- A high absentee rate—On the average, 35% of the pupils were absent each period. P.E. was a special problem area with large numbers of pupils refusing to dress down, shower, or even attend class.

- Frequent incidents of violence. One riot, for example, resulted in the burning of a police car. Outside agitators constantly fomented racial confrontations in the school.

- A high level of illegal drug use by students. Outside pushers frequented the building and grounds.

- Frequent referrals of students to the office for disciplinary action—resulting in a high rate of suspensions.

- Athletic teams which were constant losers. The football team, for example, won only three games in seven years.
- A physically unattractive cafeteria which, despite constant supervision, was the setting for a large number of disturbances. Pupils customarily left the cafeteria a mess after each lunch period.
- Low academic achievement. Large numbers of students refused to do assigned work.
- A high level of racial tension. Each of the school's seven major ethnic groups formed a highly cohesive clique. Group loyalty was to the clique, not to the school as a whole. Hostility seethed among the cliques, occasionally breaking out in violence.

Such was the situation when William Maynard became Cleveland's sixth principal in nine years. His challenge was to shape up the school or be shipped out.

THE PRINCIPAL

Bill Maynard is warm, friendly, and extroverted. He is highly energetic, enthusiastic about his work, optimistic, articulate. He shows his respect for young people by talking with them, listening to them, and sharing decisions with them. He knows how to involve them emotionally in improving their school.

He likes to implement new ideas even if some of them might be a little risky. He takes calculated, not off-the-top-of-the-head risks. Most people would call him a democratic administrator. He believes in systematic planning. He likes to share decisions with others and involve lots of people in school improvement activities.

The same year that Dr. Maynard accepted the Cleveland principalship, he also became active in a national project to define and improve school climate. The project, sponsored by CFK Ltd.,[1] defined a new role for the principal—that of initiator of school improvement projects which would change the climate of the school (1). The project also defined a number of "climate determinants"—conditions existing in the school which, if modified, would result in

---

[1] A small philanthropic foundation founded by Charles F. Kettering II. The school climate projects begun by Charles Kettering are now being continued by a non-profit voluntary organization called CADRE (Collegial Associates for Development and Renewal of Educators).

climate improvement. Some examples of climate determinants are summarized in Figure 1–1.

During the first few weeks on the job, Dr. Maynard determined that he was going to change the image of his school by launching a variety of projects to improve its climate. The sample determinants shown in Figure 1–1 are those that, over a five-year period, have been emphasized.

A Few Examples of School Climate Determinants*

Program Determinants

- Varied Learning Environments
    - The school program extends to settings beyond the school building
- Flexible Curriculum and Extracurricular Activities
    - The school's program is appropriate for ethnic and minority groups
    - Students are given alternative ways to meet curriculum requirements
    - Extracurricular activities appeal to each of the various sub-groups of students
- Rules Cooperatively Determined
    - Rules determined cooperatively with students, staff, parents and administration all participating
    - Rules are few and simple
- Active Learning
- Individualized Performance Expectations
- Varied Reward System

Process Determinants

- Problem Solving Ability
    - Problems are recognized and worked on openly
- Improvement of School Goals
    - Pupils and staff know what the goals are
    - Goals are used to provide direction for programs
- Involvement in Decision Making
    - Students, staff and administration share in making important decisions about the school
- Autonomy and Accountability
- Effective Communications

Figure 1-1

Material Determinants
- ● Suitability of the School Plant
  - ● Students and staff are proud of their plant and grounds and help keep them attractive
  - ● The building has space and physical arrangements appropriate for the school's programs

---

*Adapted from the "CFK Ltd. School Climate Profile," an instrument to measure school climate. This instrument is described in detail by the CFK Ltd. Editorial Staff, Robert Fox chairman, in that organization's book School Climate Development (1, p. 58–68). Only a small number of the determinants defined by Fox are described here.

Figure 1–1 (cont'd.)

CLEVELAND'S CLIMATE IMPROVEMENT PROJECTS

1.01 Transforming Ethnic Pride into School Pride

It took Bill only a few weeks to realize that ethnic pride within the various racial sub-groups was a potential asset. His plan was simple—and ingenious—challenge the pupils to be as proud of their school as they were of their racial identity. The first projects were to be aimed at one of the school's biggest problems—doing something about its losing football team.

At one of the first pep assemblies during his first year at Cleveland, Bill stood up in front of his students and said something like this:

> There are about 700 of us here today; and this is the first assembly that we've had in almost two years.
>
> This is supposed to be a pep assembly, and I know it's hard to find things to get excited about regarding football games. Many of you really believe that we can't win at anything. This may come as a surprise, but I believe we are winning right now, and that we are going to win big.
>
> I'll give an example. Look around you. Look at the people in front and in back of you. Many of you have been here for three years and don't even know who these people are. Many of you have never even spoken to one another. Reach out to someone new and tap them on the shoulder. Tell them they are "O.K." Just say it. "Hey   , you're O.K." See, it's easy. Besides that it feels good.
>
> That's what I meant about winning. I've been in five different schools, and I have never seen what I am seeing here. You have more pride in yourselves than I've ever seen in students anywhere. I see you in the halls, in the lunchroom, in classes and outside. The one thing that has

really impressed me is the fierce, intense pride that all of you have within your own groups.

Why don't you share it with each other? Why not reach out and touch —it's fun and it feels good. You have pride; share it.

You can start by saying it. Say "We've Got Pride." That's right, just say it. Now say it louder—Let's say it together—"We've Got Pride." Again—"We've Got Pride." Again—

Don't ever stop.

Following the assembly the "We've Got Pride" theme was adopted by the students and a number of activities and projects were organized. Some examples:

- The art department painted "I've Got Pride" on all the football helmets and the football team purchased new practice jerseys with "I've Got Pride" written on them.
- Students painted "We've Got Pride" in big letters on the wall in the main hallway.
- Three hundred beer mugs imprinted with "We've Got Pride" were purchased and sold in the school and in the community. Likewise, "We've Got Pride" buttons were printed.
- A contest was held to design a new emblem depicting an eagle, the school's mascot. Each student who submitted a design was provided paint and was allowed to put his design on the wall of the main hallway. The result was the "Hall of Eagles," a string of brightly colored designs on what had been a drab, institutional green wall.
- The following year a "Getting It Together" contest was launched. This contest was operated in much the same way as the mascot contest with pupils submitting designs for emblems portraying ethnic unity. The result was one more brightened hallway, this one dedicated to linking ethnic pride to school spirit. Figure 1–2 shows the winning design.

The "We've Got Pride" theme has continued at Cleveland, providing a kind of psychological glue which holds students and staff together. The theme has since been adopted by hundreds of other schools throughout the country.

Incidentally, as a result of the improved morale engendered by the projects, the football team began winning. During the first season the team won four games, its best season in over 20 years. The second year they went to the championship playoffs (for the first time since 1938). Cleveland's coach was named coach of the year for two years in a row. No Seattle coach had ever achieved that honor before.

Figure 1-2

Likewise, the basketball team began to win. Cleveland is the only high school in the state ever to win an AA and an AAA basketball championship in a row.

1.02 Developing an Action Plan

"School-wide improvement," says Dr. Maynard, "doesn't just happen because you want it to. You have to plan carefully."

Dr. Maynard's action plan for his first year as principal is reproduced in Appendix A.

During his first year as principal, the plan called for the accomplishment of three major goals—to provide a safe environment for kids, to improve the image of the school with the students, and to change the image of the school with the community. Those goals were continued in subsequent years but, of course, the objectives changed.

1.03 Developing an Inservice Program for Staff

Initially the Cleveland staff was highly resistant to change. Many teachers lacked the skills needed to teach successfully in a school with an open climate. Others had difficulty visualizing how climate improvement could benefit their school.

During the first three years of Dr. Maynard's tenure he and his faculty organized a wide variety of workshops, mostly dealing with the climate determinants. Sample topics:

- Improving communication skills
- Shared decision making
- Problem solving
- Group process skills

A combination of large and small group sessions was used. In some cases outside consultants were hired to provide instruments and to teach the staff skills which they needed in order to use the instruments.

One result of these sessions was the development of a Cleveland problem-solving process. This process is summarized in Figure 1–3. This process is frequently used by planning groups working on specific climate improvement projects.

Cleveland High School's Problem Solving Process

1. Write the problem down.
2. Clarify the problem. Make sure that everyone in the group understands how the problem is defined by everyone else.
3. List the indicators that the problem exists.
4. Rewrite the problem in a positive statement.
5. Brainstorm some alternative solutions to the problem.
6. Select the alternatives which are most easily implemented and most likely to succeed.
7. Write an action plan which defines who will do what. Set target dates for completion of each task.
8. Implement the action plan.
9. Evaluate what you have done.

Figure 1–3

Staff development activities continue to be an important part of Cleveland's climate improvement program. Dr. Maynard sees staff development as a major key to his success in changing the school.

1.04 Revising the Discipline Code

Very soon after Dr. Maynard's arrival at Cleveland it became apparent to him that he would not be able to function with the school's discipline code. It was so complex that pupils had trouble remembering what was in it. Also, a number of students and staff felt that it dealt with too many trivialities and placed unnecessary restrictions on students. Some of its provisions, it was felt, were unenforceable.

The new discipline code consists of only six items. It is reproduced, in its entirety, in Figure 1–4.

Cleveland High School

Seattle, Washington

DISCIPLINE CODE

1. Attend class
2. No alcohol. No drugs
3. No weapons
4. No gambling
5. No smoking in the building
6. Treat all with respect for their dignity, welfare, and material goods

---

Figure 1–4

1.05 Defining Goals

Cleveland's goals, like the discipline code, are simply stated and easily understood. Painted prominently on a corridor wall in a central location, they are read daily by hundreds of pupils. The goals are uniquely related to the school's "We've Got Pride" theme as the first letters of each goal, read vertically, spell "Pride." (See Figure 1–5.)

CLEVELAND'S GOALS

P ersonal growth and self-esteem

R espect and dignity

I ndividualized expectations

D evelopment of skills for the future

E xcitement for learning

Figure 1-5

The goals were written, with suggestions from staff and students, by Principal Bill Maynard.

1.06 Building Students' Self-Concept—Three Projects

All of Cleveland's projects contribute to the improvement of self-concept. These three, however, were organized especially for that purpose.

The Who's Who Project

This project is an on-going activity to give recognition to students and staff who do things of interest to others and of benefit to the school. The Who's Who Committee is careful to recognize a large number of individuals—not just the leaders. Recognition is given by placing a person's picture and a description of his accomplishments in one of the committee's display cases. Examples:

- "Eagles of the Month"—a display which features the contributions of individual students to school climate improvement.
- "Look Who's on the Job"—a display which gives recognition to staff members for their contributions to the school. Custodians, secretaries, and other noncertificated staff, as well as professionals, are recognized.
- "Eagles in the Field"—a display recognizing the work of students in the environmental education program.

The "Wide World of Sports"

The task force in charge of this project has charge of a large section of one corridor wall on which are displayed pictures of athletes, information about their accomplishments, and information about various athletic events. One display, for example, was built around a "Women in Sports" theme.

The Annual International Dinner

This event had been offered before Bill became principal but had always been sparsely attended. However, as the concept of ethnic pride became more central and visible this activity took on new significance, and attendance has increased significantly.

The dinner features foods unique to each ethnic group in the school. Parents, pupils and staff all work together in the planning, food preparation and serving. Following the dinner each group presents a performance representative of its own culture. A typical performance may include a Philippine bamboo dance, a traditional Japanese dance with fans and kimonos, a demonstration of *Kung Fu*, a Chinese dragon dance, a Samoan sword dance and an Afro Drum Ensemble.

Many of the performing groups have received community-wide, even city-wide recognition. They perform frequently in elementary and junior high schools, especially those schools whose pupils will be likely to come to Cleveland. They also perform for service clubs and other community groups, thus improving the image of the school in the community.

Dr. Maynard sees this activity as an important way of demonstrating that the school values ethnic diversity and supports ethnic pride. It is a means of encouraging the students to transform ethnic pride into pride in their school.

1.07 Opening Communications with an Information Booth

The student-operated information booth occupies a central location in the main hall. Students built the booth in Cleveland's construction class, and students volunteer to manage the booth during their unscheduled time.

From the booth students can obtain a wide variety of information about the school, procedures, drugs, school activities, and student rights. Students, for example, can get the student grievance forms at the booth—together with information regarding the grievance process.

Dr. Maynard is especially proud of this activity because, even though the students are not supervised, they have never betrayed the school's confidence by passing out material which would in any way be embarrassing to anyone.

1.08 Coordinating Activities with the School Climate Committee

Several school climate improvement activities are coordinated by the School Climate Committee—a group of students and staff members who meet regularly to discuss school climate problems and what to do about them. The committee periodically measures school climate, both formally and informally and suggests climate improvement activities and projects. Periodically, the committee issues a publication called the "Weather Report" which provides news of promising activities and gives recognition to individuals who have contributed to climate improvement.

1.09 Projects to Improve the Building and Grounds

Cleveland High School was built in 1923. It is not, by most standards, either an attractive or a functional building. Yet, through the efforts of lots of people, students, staff, and parents, it has been transformed into a pleasant, interesting, human place.

The initial "We've Got Pride" and "Getting It Together" contests resulted in a significant change in the appearance of the school. Those two contests stimulated a wide diversity of activity to improve the building and grounds. Examples:

- The construction class built four large umbrella-style shelters with brick patios, Greek planter boxes, tables, and benches.
- Dr. Maynard has mounted and displayed in his office five 2' × 4' color photographs of students who were selected to depict the "Spirit of Cleveland."
- Walls in all parts of the school were decorated with original student paintings. The wooden wall of a portable building has become a mural showing a bird flying into the door frame. All the mascots of all the city's high schools have been painted on the gym wall. The principal's office, the music room, and a large number of classrooms have been decorated in a similar way. The vice-principal spent part of one summer painting murals in the cafeteria. Anyone with an idea can qualify to receive paint and brushes to improve the appearance of the

school. Bare, institutional-green walls are now becoming a rarity.

- A local sculptor designed a fountain and pool for the school grounds and students helped build it. Cleveland now boasts of having the only school fountain in the state.

Involving pupils in the physical improvement of their school gives them a pride of ownership. Vandalism has almost disappeared.

1.10 Expanding the Curriculum with Minicourses

Dr. Maynard calls Cleveland's minicourse program "a major key to success" in improving student morale. Presently over 90 minicourses are offered—not all of them successful. Among the most popular are the following:

- "Improving Your Image," a six-week course to teach pupils problem solving, decision making, goal setting, and personal growth techniques. Pupils learn many of the skills which they need in order to participate in the school's decision-sharing program.
- Physical education minicourses. The entire P.E. program, once a big problem, has been reorganized into minicourses. The P.E. department now offers such courses as bowling, swimming, roller skating, golf, archery, and tennis. Eighty percent of the activities are co-ed. Ninety percent of the students enroll in P.E. even though it is no longer a required course. No other high school in the city has such a high percentage of P.E. enrollment.
- Outdoor education minicourses and activities. Many hiking, backpacking, camping, and mountain climbing experiences are offered. Cleveland groups have gone as far south as Mexico, as far east as Idaho, and as far north as Canada. Some activities are for credit; others are not. Wilderness survival, an intensive course in living off the land, is given for credit.
- Law Enforcement. This minicourse is taught by a policeman who has taken pupils to visit courtrooms and jails and has arranged for them to ride in squad cars with officers on duty. He has also introduced pupils to the canine corps and to motorcycle patrolmen. One result has been a steadily increasing enrollment of pupils in the Police Cadet Corps. Bill is fond of remembering that only a short time ago the presence of uniformed policemen on the campus was likely to trigger disturbances or violence.
- Child Care. A major activity of the participants in this minicourse is the actual operation of a day care center for a week.

The regular course structure has also been expanded to include more activity-oriented activities. For example, pupils in a construction course have just completed a project to build, with the help of community consultants, a four-place airplane.

A new career education program has also been added. Through an agreement with the Explorers organization, a wide variety of career consultants from the professions and the trades have been located. Also, a new career information center has just been opened in the school.

1.11 Modifying the Grading Policy

"Failing grades," says Dr. Maynard, "are bad for pupils' self-concept." Therefore they have been eliminated. Only credits which a pupil has earned are listed on the transcript.

Students are rewarded for the amount of work they do. They may earn ¼ credit, ½ credit, ¾ or full credit, and may receive a grade of A, B, C or D. Recently a teacher-student task force completed a new grading process. Each teacher may choose a grading style that best fits his teaching style. The four styles are: 1) A, B, C, D, no credit; 2) A, B, pass, no credit; 3) Pass, no credit; 4) Mastery—a check list based on levels of performance skills.

1.12 Sharing Decisions with Staff and Students

Recently Dr. Maynard has created a number of committees designed to involve staff and students in a wide variety of key decisions. Regarding this effort, Dr. Maynard says:

> Although not all teachers believe in this process, most of the staff and many students are very enthused about it. We have teachers and students on an interview committee for staff selection, budget development and expenditures, and almost every other function within the building. Most of us feel we are making better decisions, and there is far more commitment, support, and involvement in the implementation of our programs.

RESULTS

We have described only a few of the activities and projects which have transformed Cleveland High School. New ideas are being implemented daily. Of the 18 school climate determinants defined by Fox, significant projects were launched to affect only the twelve listed in Figure 1–1. Yet the effect on the school has been profound. Briefly, here's what has happened:

Attendance and Holding Power. The average percentage of pupils absent each period has decreased from 35% to 5.6%, the lowest percentage of any high school in the city. Cleveland's drop-out rate is also the lowest in the city.

Library Use. Library circulation has tripled in three years. In the same period the number of stolen books decreased by 70%. Book fines have been discontinued because they are no longer necessary.

Athletics. Athletic teams consistently win. Previously they consistently lost.

Requests for Transfer. School authorities used to receive more requests to transfer out of Cleveland than requests to transfer in. That ratio is now reversed.

Fights. The number of fights, both between individuals and between racial groups has decreased markedly. There were only two fights in the school last year.

Referrals to the Office. There are now 50% fewer referrals to the office than previously. Cleveland also has the lowest pupil suspension rate of any high school in the city.

Security. Discipline problems in the school have declined to such an extent that security officers are no longer assigned to the school while it is in session. Also, it is no longer necessary for staff members to be assigned to patrol halls, supervise washrooms, or monitor the cafeteria. Teachers eating with students provide casual supervision to the cafeteria area. Cleveland now averages only one security incident per year.

Assemblies. Previously assemblies could not be held because of problems with student conduct. Assemblies are now held frequently. Ten assemblies were held last year.

Increased Personal Freedom for Pupils. Pupils no longer are required to attend a supervised study hall. Instead they have a choice of leaving the campus or going to the library or the cafeteria. The increase in action-type learning activities, contract learning, and independent study necessitates more student movement. This increase in student freedom has not resulted in an increase in discipline problems.

Problems With Nonstudents. Outsiders coming into the school to sell dope or otherwise cause trouble are still a problem. Recently, however, Cleveland students have been informing outsiders that they are not welcome and have been telling them to stay out of the building.

Outside Agencies. Anyone in a uniform coming into the school used to be subjected to threats and insults. Military recruiters and uniformed police now visit the building regularly with no serious problems. They are, in fact, welcomed and treated courteously.

Publicity. The school used to receive a combination of bad publicity and no publicity at all. However, the school recently averaged four feature news articles and two TV reports on its program each year. As principal, Bill Maynard has been asked to speak at a number of national conventions, thus spreading good publicity nationwide.

Academic Achievement.

- Sixty percent of Cleveland's graduating class now enrolls in college—up from 35% five years ago.

- The number of National Merit Scholarship finalists has increased by 50% in the past three years.

- The number of students receiving scholarships to college has increased.

Obviously Bill Maynard had never read this book when he began his reform of Cleveland High School. Yet much of what he did is in accord with what we recommend in Chapters 2–8.

He shaped up his cafeteria and simplified, defined, and publicized the school's rules as we recommend in Chapter 2. He opened communications among cliques and modified his grading policies as we suggest in Chapter 5. As suggested in Chapter 6, he greatly expanded the extracurricular programs by enhancing ethnic pride and awareness, by expanding performing groups, by involving students in improving the appearance of the building, by honoring and rewarding more students, by offering morale-building assemblies, and by operating "We've Got Pride" task forces. As we suggest in Chapter 7, he expanded the curriculum by offering a variety of mini-courses, by initiating action learning programs, by involving pupils with curriculum planning, by involving community resources in instruction, and by providing alternative learning environments. He also initiated a course of instruction in values, and, in his own way, in morals.

He did all of this, and more, as a part of a unified program to improve his school's climate.

For the past five years Cleveland has been proving to the city of Seattle and to the nation that inner city high schools can be pleasant, exciting, humane places. Bill Maynard has done more than just improve discipline at Cleveland High School. He has basically changed the school by modifying only a few of its climate determinants.

If you would like further information regarding the climate improvement concept you might do two things:

1) Order the CFK Ltd. book, *School Climate Improvement,* from Phi Delta Kappa.[2]

2) Order the catalog of publications of CFK Ltd. and CADRE, available free of charge from the Nueva Learning Center, P.O. Box 1366, Burlingame, CA 94010.

With the instruments available in the CFK Ltd. book you will be ready to diagnose the climate in your own school and to begin planning projects which will make a difference. The result will be two-fold: (1) an improvement in student and staff morale and productivity and (2) a sharp reduction of discipline problems.

---

[2]Phi Delta Kappa, Inc., 8th and Union Streets, Bloomington, IN 47401, $3.00 per copy. (Payment must accompany orders of less than $6.00.)

Shaping Up the School I–
Conducting a Campaign
Against Crime and Violence

2

Our goal is to make our schools good places for the children and adults in them. They must be places where people can live and grow and learn to love learning, where people can learn to respect themselves and to care a lot about one another. Such a humane school, however, cannot be built in an atmosphere of lawlessness and disorder.

There need not be a conflict between the humanistic approach and the law and order approach to improving discipline. A school which is run by the staff instead of by lawless gangs of youths is not necessarily a joyless, nondemocratic place. On the contrary, pupils can learn creatively and enthusiastically only if a reasonable level of orderliness is maintained.

This chapter, Chapter 3, and Chapter 4 provide a variety of suggestions for establishing a minimal level of stability in a school. Then, given a relatively peaceful atmosphere, you and your staff can begin work on the causes of discipline problems, many of which are deeply rooted in the nature of the school itself.

TWELVE WAYS TO SHAPE UP A SCHOOL

2.01 Developing Your Action Plan

Our first suggestion to you, as you develop a program to reduce violence and vandalism, is to develop an action plan. This plan should include at least four sections, as follows:

(1) A definition of the plan's objectives stated clearly enough so that they can be measured. Examples:

● The cost of vandalism to this school will be reduced from the present cost of $2.77 per student to $1.00 per student.[1]

● The number of student assaults will be reduced by 10% in one year and the degree of severity of the assaults will decrease.

(2) The plan will specify the activities which will lead to the achievement of the objectives, and the responsibility for the success of each activity will be assigned. Examples:

● The Board of Education will provide funds in the budget for a night alarm system.

● The student council will sponsor a series of "We've Got Pride" assemblies and a project to expand the extra-curricular program to attract more students.

(3) The plan will specify how each objective will be evaluated. Example:

● Information regarding the number and severity of assaults will be documented on the discipline report forms currently in use by the assistant principal. A faculty-student committee will rate the degree of severity of the assaults and will issue an end-of-the-year report on its findings.

(4) The plan will include a budget.

Figure 2–1 summarizes the four essential components of an action plan and poses several key questions related to each component.

Parents, pupils, staff, and, perhaps, local law enforcement officers should be involved in the planning. Prior to beginning their work, the committee members should be pledged to help implement the plan. Otherwise, your committee may fall into the usual trap of spending a lot of time and energy thinking up things for someone else (usually the principal) to do. It is essential that task forces or individuals be assigned responsibility for each activity, that tasks be clearly defined and deadlines agreed upon.

A large number of excellent suggestions for activities for your plan can be found in a recent publication of the National School Public Relations Association entitled *Violence and Vandalism—Current Trends in School Policies and Programs* (8). We recommend that your task force use that publication, along with this book, as a basic reference.

---

[1] Note: This objective was actually achieved by a Colorado school.

Essential Components of an Action Plan

1. Objectives
   - What do we want to happen?
2. Activities
   - Who will do what when?
3. Evaluation
   - How will we know what happened and why?
4. Budget
   - How much will the plan cost?
   - Will the plan save the school any money?

Figure 2-1

2.02 Organize a Student Security Advisory Committee

Such committees have been effective in many districts, including Prince George's County Maryland. At Parkdale High School (12) where student committee members monitor the parking lot, thefts from cars have been reduced from 35 a month to almost zero. Parkdale's committee has 400 members. It is important that pupils understand their roles as members of such an organization and that they be carefully trained. At Parkdale the students understand that they are there as "observers." Their job is to "use their eyes and ears to make the school a better and safer place." They are not asked to inform on their friends and are not authorized to put their hands on anybody.

"Having students on your side," says committee sponsor Peter Blauvelt, "is the only way I know to make schools safe."

2.03 Implementing a Financial Incentive Program

Several school districts have reported substantial vandalism cost reductions as a result of this idea. At South San Francisco's Unified School District (13), each of the district's twenty schools is provided a kitty equal in dollars to the school's average daily attendance, (e.g., a school with an ADA of 500 pupils is granted $500). During the second semester the dollar cost of each school's vandalism is deducted from the kitty of the school. Whatever is left can be spent by student committees on school improvements. District officials report that as a result of this program, vandalism costs have been reduced from $33,000 per year to $7,000. Similar programs have been successful in Colville, Washington, where vandalism was reduced by 90% in one year, and in Louisville, Kentucky. In Louisville the School Board set aside 20 cents per student to be used at each school's discretion with the understanding that any reduction in vandalism cost over the previous year would be added to the grant money. Vandalism costs plunged. A similar program operates in Roanoke, Virginia, and Meeker, Colorado. Meeker's policy statement describing their program is reproduced in Figure 2–2. Mapleton School District #1, serving several Denver suburban communities, has defined its vandalism reduction program in the district's administrative regulations. These regulations, which show in detail how the program functions, are reproduced in Appendix B.

MEEKER STUDENT SCHOOL BOARD MAINTENANCE FUND

Meeker, Colorado

There is hereby created a sum of money to be known as the Student-School Board Maintenance Fund. This is an annual fund to be divided between the Meeker Junior High ($100.00) and the Meeker High School ($400.00).

Its purpose is to gain the help of the Meeker students in properly maintaining the Meeker School Facilities.

On the last day of the school year this fund in separate high school and junior high divisions will be divided equally among the classes involved *minus* any monies spent from the fund to replace lost items of school property, to repair needless damage to school property, or to clean up after needless littering of school property.

Figure 2–2

2.04 Beefing Up Your Building's Security—
Seventeen Ideas

The most obvious and usual way to improve your building's security is through the employment of a security staff. These individuals need not be policemen. They should, however, be well-trained in surveillance and in investigative techniques. A small staff that can solve crimes and prosecute young criminals is more cost effective than a larger staff engaged primarily in supervision. Some additional ideas:

● Start a "trailer watchers program."

Set aside space on the school ground for a trailer and provide housing rent-free to residents. They, in return, report all suspicious activity to the principal or to the police. This idea originated in the Elk Grove (California) Unified School District, located in a rural area near Sacramento (16). Vandalism and break-ins virtually ceased at the district's 17 schools. A similar program is in operation in the Escambie County Schools, Pensacola, Florida.

● Do a security audit (6, p. 64).

Such a study is designed to evaluate existing security procedures, security roles of all personnel, security equipment and the safety and vulnerability of buildings, and services available from outside agencies such as the police and fire departments. A key part of the security audit is the analysis of records that show which buildings are most vulnerable and at which times of the day, days of the week, and months of the year most vandalism occurs. Based on the findings of the audit a district-wide security action plan can be developed.

● Launch a "School Neighbor Project."

A growing number of schools are enlisting the aid of residents in the school neighborhood in preventing break-ins and vandalism of school property. Typically the principal goes to each home in the immediate neighborhood, introduces himself, and requests the neighbors to report any suspicious activity either to the police or to the principal. Callers may remain anonymous. The Englewood, Colorado program provides for cash rewards of up to $100 to neighbors who report suspicious-looking intruders on school property. One result of the Englewood program was a 90% reduction in window breakage costs. An effective program is also in operation in Cleveland (15). Fairfax County (Virginia) Public Schools distribute handy reference cards to residents of homes located near schools. Figure 2–3 is a reproduction of the front of the card. On the reverse side (Figure 2–4) a letter of the district's division superintendent asks for each neighbor's help in reducing the district's $307,000 vandalism bill.

● Use electronic devices for improved security (11).

Electronic devices can be very helpful, but also very expensive, as a way of reducing violence and vandalism. In some cases, for very little cost, a school's existing public address system can be converted into an after-hours alarm system. Jefferson County, Kentucky, a large (102 schools) system, converted its existing public address systems at the approximate cost of $800 per school. Subsequently vandalism costs plunged from $150,000 per year to $33,000.

Other, more sophisticated and expensive devices can be installed which are sensitive to changes in temperature and which automatically flash a warning on a console in the police or fire station. Part of the cost of installing effective equipment may be offset by a reduction in insurance rates.

In Fulton County (Atlanta), Georgia, for example, insurance rates related to security have dropped 10% each year for the past two years. School officials there estimate that their microwave sensor system has eliminated 80 to 90% of the vandalism and theft when buildings are unoccupied.

● Institute a "no cash after hours" policy in all of your district's schools (13, p. 36). The policy should be widely publicized and summarized on decals placed on each building's outside doors. In Decatur, Illinois the decals read:

> "No money is left in this building. All cash is removed and deposited in the bank at the close of the school each day."

In Decatur this policy resulted in a drastic lowering of the number of school break-ins.

● Other security improvements might include:

1) Keep expensive equipment in a vault or in secure cabinets. Securely anchor small safes to the floor.

2) Stencil or engrave expensive equipment with your school name. If your local police has an equipment-engraving program, register such items with the police.

3) Eliminate climbable appendages on buildings.

4) Replace old, obsolete, easy-to-force door locks.

Figure 2-3

Fairfax County Public Schools
10700 Page Avenue, Fairfax, Virginia 22030

October 20, 1975

Dear Neighbor:

Are you aware that vandalism in your public schools cost Fairfax County taxpayers $307,000 last year? That's enough to hire 29 to 34 more teachers or renovate two schools or buy 28 new school buses!

We've taken a number of steps in the last few years to stem the rising cost of vandalism, including the installation of an electronic detection system in all schools, providing roving security patrols and effecting the fullest possible cooperation with county and local police.

We need your help to lower the cost of vandalism!

The school in sight of your home, or one you may be passing, is one of those damaged by vandals. Perhaps you have noticed persons on the school grounds who were behaving suspiciously, or even actually engaging in vandalism, but you did not know where to call or did not want to get involved.

The information on the reverse side of this card tells how you can help us reduce the waste of our tax dollars on vandalism. Please save this card; keep it handy by your telephone. If you notice anything suspicious going on at a school, follow the instructions on the card. You can help without having to give your name.

If you would like to know more about our school security program, call the security office at 691-2600, between 8 a.m. and 4 p.m. weekdays.

Sincerely

S. John Davis
Division Superintendent

Figure 2-4

5) Improve the lighting of your school grounds.

6) Install heavy screening over your most valuable glass areas.

7) Employ night watchmen or schedule custodial crews to work all night.

8) Install security fences in vulnerable areas.

9) Arrange for more frequent police patrols of all school buildings.

10) Encourage community use of the building at night and during the summer. Occupied buildings are less susceptible to vandalism than are unoccupied buildings.

11) Publicize the cost of vandalism in an annual report to the public. Ask assistance from the public in reducing the cost.

12) Make a special plea to persons who own citizens band radios. Ask them to use their radios any time they see suspicious activity around schools.

Many school districts can verify that ideas such as those just suggested can significantly reduce vandalism. For example, Superintendent Bernard "Pat" Ryan of Boulder, Colorado, has reported a reduction of vandalism costs of over 70% in two years (from $65,000 to $18,600). He accomplished this by implementing several of the security ideas just enumerated.

2.05 Fifteen Suggestions for Shaping Up Your School Building

Much can be done to make a building less prone to vandalism. Following are several ideas which have worked in a variety of places:

1) Take tempting targets out of washrooms. Fairfax County, Virginia put wash fountains and towel dispensers in the halls where they can be more easily supervised (14, p. 44).

2) Remove doors from toilet stalls in secondary schools. Also remove corridor doors to washrooms and provide privacy by installing panels. Eliminate bars over stall doorways.

3) Replace metal partitions with masonry.

4) Recess as many fixtures as possible throughout the building but especially in washrooms and in the cafeteria.

5) Insist that your custodial and maintenance staffs repair or replace broken fixtures, furniture, and equipment immediately.

You may have to harrass your staff in order for this to happen. It helps to have a readily available stockpile of spare parts and replacements for frequently damaged items. You can help your maintenance people by helping them plan their work, by running interference for them with the central office, and by praising their efforts.

6) Use the Christmas and summer holidays to make major improvements in the appearance of your building. Every effort should be made to get your building in near-perfect shape when pupils return from summer and winter vacations.

7) Apply ceramic-type hard-surface paint in all highly vulnerable areas.

8) Paint lockers bright colors and remove marks from the newly painted surfaces daily.

9) Install a "graffiti board," combined, perhaps, with an announcement board.

10) Replace your most frequently broken windows with acrylic plastic or similar hard-to-break material. Be careful, however, not to use easy-to-scratch materials that's another problem.

11) Encourage individual students, art students, and student organizations to paint murals throughout the school. Give each art student one ceiling tile to paint and replace in the corridor.

12) Sponsor clean-up, pick-up, and fix-up days and involve parents, pupils and staff in brightening up your building. The 5th and 6th grade girls, for example, in the Indian Grove School, Mt. Prospect, Illinois, cleaned, repainted and decorated their washroom. Principal Joe Wawak reports that the room looks great.

13) Involve student and parent organizations in fund raising projects for special, extra building projects. For example, pupils at the Cleveland High School in Seattle built a fountain. Parents at Urbana, Illinois' Leal School redesigned the school's playground. A few pieces of carpeting and some draperies here and there can make a big difference.

14) Sponsor tree planting days in the spring.

15) Asphalt or pave parking areas. Gravel provides a non-ending supply of rocks for breaking glass.

These are but a few ideas; your students, staff members, and parents can think up many more. How your building looks is an important determinant of morale. Once a building starts going downhill it is very hard to reverse the process. But, with everyone's help, it can be done.

2.06 Employing Specialists in Dealing with Disruptive Students

Such a specialist, according to Raymond Bell of Lehigh University (2, p. 57) should have three general areas of competence: "diagnostic and remedial teaching competence; crisis intervention skills; and a thorough knowledge of the community, particularly agencies from which their clients seek help." Bell's suggestions are reproduced in Figure 2–5.

2.07 Organizing a "Parents on Patrol" Program

Volunteer parents can be enlisted to help supervise children, especially young children on the way to school or on the way home. They can also be helpful at any school function where large numbers of people are present and as assistants in supervising playgrounds, hallways, and washrooms. One such program has been organized by an NAACP chapter in some of Chicago's West Side neighborhoods (9, p. 28). Their presence on street corners around 135 West Side schools deters youth gangs from accosting children. The volunteers wear distinctive caps and badges but no uniforms.

2.08 Do Something About Bomb Threats and False Fire Alarms

Bomb threats and false fire alarms plague most schools. They are visible evidence of the extent of lawlessness in our society. We suggest that you form a task force[2] in your school to study and solve the problem. Some solutions that have worked:

● The Fairfield, Connecticut schools have developed a tape cartridge which records all incoming calls. It will automatically erase all nonthreatening calls within three minutes. When a threatening call is received, however, the tape is preserved as evidence.

---

[2]Please note the difference between a task force and a committee. A task force is a group which defines a problem, then acts to solve it. A committee usually just studies a problem and thinks up things for other people (usually the principal) to do.

THE CRISIS INTERVENTION TEACHER

List of Dos and Don'ts*

DON'T:

- let the crisis-intervention teacher think he replaces a counselor or any other specialist.
- expect him to operate in a traditional mode—usually these have already failed with the population with whom he works.
- expect him to solve all the problems of all the students in your school.
- expect him to be a policeman or disciplinarian.
- place him in competition or in conflict with other teaching faculty. If he succeeds, it will be because he is trained to deal with the students that are having difficulty and not because other teachers have necessarily failed.
- overload him with so many students he can't solve anyone's problem. His case load should rarely exceed 20 students at any given time.

DO:

- have a clearly understood idea of what his role is and see that everyone else understands it, too.
- expect him to work outside the school building and outside school hours.
- be aware that when such teachers deal with these students in a relatively nontraditional role there will inevitably be conflicts at all levels. Be prepared for them.
- recognize the need for administrative support. Dealing with alienated students in crisis situations on a regular basis and coordinating a multiplicity of agency efforts is a remarkably draining job. Anyone doing it needs regular reinforcement. They expect it and ought to receive it from you.

*Reproduced by permission of the author, Dr. Raymond Bell, Director, Social Restoration Program, Lehigh University, Bethlehem, Pennsylvania.

Figure 2–5

● Michigan's Ypsilanti High School's principal (1) has developed a procedure for receiving calls which cuts down on the number of times the building must be evacuated. The school person taking each call records the call and attempts to get answers to a series of pre-determined questions. The building is then searched with the search concentrating on a list of twelve "possible bomb locations." While the search is under way the police arrive and participate in the decision regarding evacuation of the building. This decision is then made on the basis of previously agreed-upon criteria.

As you and your task force define your own criteria for clearing a building you might use consultants from your police and fire departments and from the telephone company.

Telephone company representatives can also help the task force work out procedures for tracing telephone calls.

The National School Public Relations Association (8, p. 40), quoting a U.S. Government publication, suggests that any plan for handling bomb threats should contain six elements:

1) Establish clear-cut levels of authority at the building and district level (who makes what kinds of decisions?)

2) Provide for an emergency control center

3) List emergency numbers, such as the fire department and other local agencies with bomb disposal units

4) Provide for building inspection in case of a threat. Compile a list of possible hiding places for bombs

5) Develop plans for evacuating the building

6) Provide, in the plan, information regarding bomb search techniques

An excellent basic resource for your task force is "Bomb Threats and Search Techniques" (3), from which the above was excerpted

For reducing the number of false fire alarms in your school, you might try this procedure:

1) Get a policy statement from your Board of Education that any pupil turning in a false alarm in a school will be expelled and prosecuted. Discuss with your board the implications of the policy (e.g., a board member's children or his friend's child may be the first one caught).

2) Publicize the statement widely.

3) Confer with police officers and the district attorney immedi-

ately after the policy is adopted. The purpose of the conference is to inform them of the Board's determination to stop
the false alarms and to secure their cooperation in investiga-
tion and prosecution.

4) Meet with the total school staff, inform them of what you
   have done, and ask their cooperation in detecting violators.
   Assure the staff that violators will be prosecuted.

5) Meet with the student council and other student organizations for the same purpose.

6) If your staff apprehends a student turning in a false alarm,
   have him arrested, prosecuted, and expelled.

If the preceding steps are carefully followed the number of
false fire alarms in your building will be drastically reduced or
eliminated. Be prepared, however, to actually follow through on the
expulsions and prosecutions. This is unpleasant but effective. This
procedure was followed in part by the Urbana, Illinois High School
with very positive results.

A less drastic procedure for reducing false alarms comes from
Mr. Ben Canada, Principal of the Sharples Junior High School in
Seattle. At a cost of about $6.00 per unit for materials, Sharples cus-
todians enclosed alarm handles in small steel boxes with glass windows. A hammer hangs on a chain outside the box. Thus, an individual,
to sound the alarm, must break the glass on the outside box before
he can pull the alarm handle. Mr. Canada reports that this extra step
in the process of sounding an alarm has discouraged students from
setting off the alarm just for kicks. He also reports that false alarms
are no longer a problem in his school.

Similar devices have been installed by the custodians at the
Ridgewood High School in Norridge, Illinois, with similar results.

2.09 Developing a Student Code of Rights and Responsibilities

The development of a student code is frequently one of the first
activities of a discipline committee. Such codes are helpful in defining student and staff rights and responsibilities, the laws of the state
governing students, and the policies of the Board of Education. They
can clarify for all concerned what is meant by "student rights" and
"due process" in a given school.

Committees wishing to develop a code might begin by studying the "Sample Student Code" developed by Phi Delta Kappa's Commission on Administrative Behaviors Supportive of Human Rights (4).

An especially concise, well-worded statement, developed by the parents and staff of the Leal School, Urbana, Illinois, is reproduced in Figure 2–6.

Leal School

Urbana, Illinois

LEAL RIGHTS AND RESPONSIBILITIES

My Rights	*My Responsibilities*
I have a right to be happy and to be treated with compassion in this school: this means that no one will laugh at me or hurt my feelings.	I have the responsibility to treat others with compassion: this means that I will not laugh at others, tease others, or try to hurt the feelings of others.
I have the right to be myself in this school: this means that no one will treat me unfairly because I am black or white,	I have the responsibility to respect others as individuals and not to treat others unfairly because they are black or white,
fat or thin boy or girl	
tall or short adult or child	fat or thin boy or girl
	tall or short adult or child
I have the right to be safe in this school: this means that no one will	I have the responsibility to make the school safe by not
hit me pinch me	
kick me threaten me	hitting anyone pinching anyone
push me hurt me	kicking anyone threatening anyone
	pushing anyone hurting anyone
I have the right to expect my property to be safe in this school.	I have the responsibility not to steal or destroy the property of others.
I have the right to hear and be heard in this school: this means that no one will	I have the responsibility to help maintain a calm and quiet school: this means I will not
yell make loud noises	
scream or otherwise disturb me	yell make loud noises
shout	scream or otherwise disturb others
	shout

Figure 2-6

I have the right to learn about myself and others in this school: this means that I will be free to express my feelings and opinions without being interrupted or punished.

I have the right to be helped to learn self-control in this school: this means that no one will silently stand by while I abuse the rights of others or when others abuse my rights.

I have the right to expect that all these rights will be mine in all circumstances so long as I am exercising my full responsibilities.

I have the responsibility to learn about myself and others in this school: this means that I will be free to express my feelings and opinions without being interrupted or punished and I will not interrupt or punish others who express their feelings and opinions.

I have the responsibility to learn self-control in this school: this means I will strive to exercise my rights without denying the same rights to others and I will expect to be corrected when I do abuse the rights of others as they shall be corrected if my rights are abused.

I have the responsibility to protect my rights and the rights of others by exercising my full responsibilities in all circumstances.

Figure 2-6 (cont'd.)

The National School Public Relations Association, in a recent pamphlet (7), recommends that student codes should contain at least three sections:

- Student rights
- Rules of conduct and sanctions for violations, and
- Regulations for procedural due process in matters involving suspension, transfer, and expulsion

Following is an example, from the Philadelphia Board of Education, of the type of statement that might be found in Part III of the code:

Any individual who commits a violent or other criminal act on school property shall be removed from the school premises immediately. Individuals who commit such crimes as assault, carrying a deadly weapon, threat to do bodily harm, sales or use of drugs, alcohol, or other illegal commodity; robbery (including shakedown and extortion); or any offense viewed by the administrator in charge as being sufficiently serious shall be immediately suspended. (7, p. 33.)

Indications are that school districts without well-defined codes may be in trouble if they are ever involved in a court suit. Without a code a district may be forced to follow guidelines defined by the court.

2.10 Organizing a Conflict Resolution Program

Social psychologists John P. De Cecco and Arlene K. Richards advocate that procedures be developed in schools for adults and students to engage in serious negotiations of the causes of conflict. The proposed process would consist of three basic steps (5, p. 56).

1. All parties to a conflict state their versions of the issues, expressing their anger verbally if they want to.
2. They agree on a common statement of the issues to be negotiated.
3. They bargain so that each side makes gains and concessions, and they make definite plans to carry out their agreements.

Such a process, because it is time consuming, might best be reserved primarily for crisis prevention. At a time, however, when the lid is about to blow, you might use the process to bring leaders of conflicting groups together to negotiate their differences. Use of the process could be especially helpful in preventing gang conflicts or racial conflicts in the school.

You might experiment with the process on some minor issues first so that you understand how to use the process when a crisis seems to be building.

A common organizational device for providing for conflict resolution is the establishment of an interagency team at the school building level. Such teams generally are staffed with school counselors, social workers, psychologists, fire and police officers, probation officers, and other community leaders who work regularly with children and youth. Their job may include sponsoring human relations and conflict resolution training for faculties, offering instruction on law enforcement to pupils, resolving community problems which may cause tensions among student cliques, and sponsoring service projects to up-grade neighborhoods. Such groups are especially valuable in communities where racial tensions are high. Successful programs are in operation in Pasadena, San Diego, Yerba Buena (San Jose), and several other California communities (10, p. 26).

One unique conflict resolution program, at Denny Junior High School in Seattle, has drastically reduced the number of fights in the school. Here's how the program works:

Each year principal Warren Arnhart and Assistant Principal Jack Duranceau appoint twenty-one students to membership on the school's "Rumor and Conflict Control Committee." (Actually a task force.) Mr. Duranceau reports that he likes to select the school's "unelected leaders" to this group—students who are highly respected and recognized in their respective cliques. Every effort is made to see that as many cliques as possible are represented on the committee. Some committee members have been discipline problems; all members are influential.

When any member of the committee hears a rumor of a fight starting, that member informs Mr. Duranceau of the situation. Two members of the committee are then called out of class to meet with the individuals who have a conflict. The conflict resolution meetings take place in Room 101, an abandoned teachers' lounge. No adult is present during the sessions. The students are expected to remain in Room 101 until the conflict is solved. Students are provided no formal training in conflict resolution processes; they are simply expected to talk out the problem and report to Mr. Duranceau when the matter has been settled.

Conflicts which have been resolved have ranged from name-calling and hair-pulling to more serious offenses such as extortion and fist fights. Most conflicts are settled before a blow is struck. Mr. Duranceau reports that students have even settled longstanding community feuds with this process. One student's comment: "We've got things completely under control."

Mr. Arnhart is enthusiastic about the results of the program. He has one reservation about it, however. He's concerned that a high level of trust needs to be built between pupils and the assistant principal before such a program can be organized. "If they don't trust the guy who runs it," says Mr. Arnhart, "the program won't function."

2.11 Ten Ideas for Improving Your Cafeteria

In elementary as well as secondary schools, the cafeteria is often seen as a breeding place for discipline problems. If violence is going to happen in a school there is a good chance that it will happen in a cafeteria. It is true that many cafeterias are not very pleasant places. Elementary school cafeterias often operate in rooms designed for primary use as gymnasiums. Pupils sit at long tables, eating military style. The area is frequently supervised by para-professionals whose knowledge of child behavior is limited. The room is typically drab and noisy; the climate is too often either chaotic or repressive.

Secondary school cafeterias, even though they may have been designed as eating places, are seldom more pleasant. The potential for violence, however, is greater.

As a first step in improving your cafeteria you might form a task force—an action-oriented group of staff members, pupils, and parents who are willing to define and solve the problem. Once the problem is defined, the group may wish to consider some of these solutions:

1) Improve the place physically. Do wall murals. Launch a **PTA** project to buy some drapes or new furniture. Replace some gang feeding tables with smaller ones (the group size for eating tranquilly should not exceed four). Develop an outside eating area for use in good weather. Revamp the lighting system. Install sound-deadening acoustical panels.

2) Organize a noon-hour activity program. One school we know offers a different sports experience for pupils in the gym each week. Other schools schedule club meetings and other activities over the noon hour.

3) Conduct an inservice program for the cafeteria supervisors. Arrange for the supervisors to meet periodically with a faculty sponsor and a group of pupils to discuss problems and solutions.

4) Enlist the aid of student service groups to help keep the cafeteria clean.

5) Modify the school's schedule so that long lines are made shorter and so that the total number of pupils in the room at one time is reduced to the lowest possible number.

6) Form a menu-planning committee. Such a committee not only provides an opportunity for student involvement in school management, it also can provide valuable learning experiences in finance and nutrition.

7) Start a breakfast program and encourage teachers to eat breakfast with students. There is evidence that in many schools breakfast programs reduce student absenteeism.

8) Review the rules of conduct for students in the cafeteria.

Eliminate the unenforceable ones and devise ways to enforce those remaining in an unobtrusive, routine manner.

9) Start a "We're Proud of Our Cafeteria" publicity campaign with posters, school paper articles, class meetings, and assemblies.

10) Provide for a method of isolating chronic trouble-makers.

You may wish to rotate membership on your task force periodically so that a large number of pupils can participate. It is important that pupils begin to feel proud of their cafeteria. This will happen as they become actively involved in its improvement.

2.12 Start a Campaign to Improve Discipline on School Buses

Lots of discipline problems and some lawlessness and violence occur on school buses. One common difficulty is the lack of training of bus drivers to understand and work with children and youth. Another may be a lack of clearly defined procedures. The bus driver may, for example, be unsure of his authority.

It is important that drivers be provided with inservice training to help them build and maintain positive relationships with their passengers. Such sessions might be organized by your task force on school bus discipline.

The Mounds View, Minnesota School District devised the "Tips for Maintaining Discipline" list reproduced in Figure 2–7. Your task force may want to revise this list and discuss it with your drivers at one or more of the inservice sessions.

Some additional ideas:

1) Install a Super 8 monitor camera in some buses. The driver can activate such a camera without stopping the bus. Thus a photographic record of discipline problems is available. Farmington, Maine's School District #9 has a number of cameras in use. Cost was $259.80 per unit.

2) Devise and publicize a procedure for removing bus riding privileges from disruptive students.

3) Keep, in the school's discipline office, complete records of discipline infractions on the buses.

We are clearly advocating in this chapter a no-nonsense approach to improving discipline in the school. We do so because of our concern for the welfare of the millions of children in our schools who

Tips to Bus Drivers on Maintaining Discipline*

The very act of stopping the bus to reprimand a pupil lends emphasis to the situation. When speaking to the offender, driver should speak in a courteous manner but with a firm voice. There should be no anger involved. A driver should not let his personal problems reflect themselves in his mood or judgment while dealing with his passengers. If necessary, the student should be moved to a seat near the driver. A pupil should never be put off the bus enroute to walk home.

A few tips on maintaining discipline:

- Never give an order you do not mean to enforce; give a student time to react.

- The response of the student is in action. Give your command to stimulate action, not to check it. Say, do this, rather than don't do that. Suggest an action which can be successfully obeyed.

- Have a reason for what you ask a child to do, and when possible take time to give the reason—he can see the point if you can.

- Be honest in what you say and do. Be fair; it isn't punishment, but injustice that makes a child rebel against you. A child's faith in you is a great help.

- Commend good qualities and action; all children have them.

- Try to be constructive, not repressive, in all dealings with children.

- Remember that a sense of humor is extremely valuable.

- You may never strike a student passenger, or physically abuse same.

- Do not judge misconduct on how it annoys you. Do not take your personal feelings and prejudices out on the children. Maintain poise at all times. Do not lose your temper.

- Remember the tongue is the only keen edge tool which grows sharper with constant use. Do not nag, bluff, or be officious.

- Do not pick on every little thing a child does. Sometimes it is wiser to overlook some things.

- Be sincere in your work and set a good example yourself. Intelligence in handling youth consists of thinking faster than they do. If they can out think you, you are not using your maturity and the advantage of your larger education. You should see possibilities before they become results. This is the secret of leadership.

---

*Courtesy of Mounds View, Minnesota, School District.

Figure 2-7

are not discipline problems. These children deserve an orderly environment in which to grow and learn. They deserve to be free from fear of violence and from juvenile crime, and their parents, who are paying for the schools, need to have increased confidence in the schools their children attend.

Shaping Up a School II—
Handling Discipline Problems Effectively

3

Much that a school administrator does to improve the school deals not so much with preventing violence and lawlessness as with operating the school in an efficient, humane manner. One good place to start is in the administrative offices. The school administrator himself—how he handles routine, how he talks to people, how he solves problems—determines to a great extent whether or not the school will be orderly.

VISIBILITY

It is important that the school administrator be visible and that he show an interest in the pupils and the staff. People in the school need to feel that the administrator cares enough about them to listen to them, to know their names, to help them out if they have problems.

Dr. Kimball Howes, former principal at Lakewood High School in Lakewood and Southeast High School in Ravenna, Ohio, has these suggestions for making yourself visible:

● Stand on the sidewalk in front of the school each morning as students are arriving and ask the assistant principal (if you have one) to do the same. Say hello to pupils as they arrive. This practice not only demonstrates friendliness, it also alleviates problems of smoking, tardiness, and loitering outside the building. Adults driving by the school or driving pupils to the school are impressed favorably.

● Manage your time so that at least 25% of the day is spent in hallways, the cafeteria, the lounge, and in classrooms.

● Eat in the student lunchroom yourself and talk to students.

● Be serious about an open door policy, especially if a pupil is upset about something. Instruct your secretary to let you know at once when a student who is upset comes into the office.

● Know as many of your pupil's names as possible. Learn something about their families, their interests, and their activities. Talking to a pupil when he's not in trouble improves your effectiveness with him when he is in trouble.

ADMINISTERING DISCIPLINE PROBLEMS EFFICIENTLY

Improving the administration of discipline problems is a necessary step in shaping up the school as a whole. Discipline records must be accurate, complete, fair, and legal. The causes of discipline problems must be studied and solutions implemented; the attendance system must operate efficiently; and referred pupils from teachers must be seen promptly and treated fairly.

Following are nine ways to improve the administrative procedures for handling discipline and attendance problems in your school.

3.01 Improve Your System for Recording Disciplinary Infractions

Whenever a student is sent to the office for disciplinary reasons a record should be made of the referral.

Figure 3–1 shows a suggested form for keeping a record of pupil referrals. Parts 1, 2, 3, and 4 should be filled out by the teacher at the time the referral is made and the form should accompany the student when he goes to the office. In this way the administrator has available a written summary of the incident or problem while he talks to the pupil.

The form is filled out in duplicate so that the administrator can send a report of his action to the teacher as soon as that action is completed. The referral procedures, detailed on the back of the form (See Figure 3–2) assure teachers that they will receive a report of action taken within 24 hours.

(Sample)

The _____ School

Anecdotal Referral Form

Date ____
Time ____

1. Student's name: _____

2. Referred by: _____

3. Description of Incident Observed or Problem:

4. Action taken by teacher:

5. Is administrative action requested?   ☐ Yes   ☐ No

6. Action taken by administrator:

7. Student's statement (may be appended to this form)

_____   _____
Student's signature   Administrator's signature

Figure 3–1

A somewhat different referral form is suggested by Mr. James K. Sledge, administrative assistant at Brooklyn Park High School in Baltimore (Figure 3–3).

One of the most important areas on the form is a space for the teacher to request a conference with the student with the adminis-

Procedures for Using the Anecdotal Referral Form

1. Teachers are encouraged to take action regarding the pupil's behavior prior to referral. Such action may include contacting the parent, a teacher-pupil conference, or referral to the counseling office. This action may be reported to the administration on an anecdotal referral form with an indication that administrative action is not requested.

2. If a teacher requests that administrative action be taken a response to that request will be given within 24 hours.

3. Teachers are encouraged to discuss observations, problems, or referrals as soon as possible after submission of this form.

4. Parents and pupils are encouraged to review the pupil's discipline record periodically and may file statements of their own if they wish to do so.

5. Positive as well as negative information about a pupil should be submitted. Of special importance to the record are reports of successful attempts by the pupil to improve his behavior.

6. Anecdotal referral forms will be removed from the record no later than three years after the date of the referral.

Figure 3-2

trator present. According to Mr. Sledge there are many advantages to such conferences. He suggests that the role of the administrator be that of a mediator rather than that of an umpire.

"The form," says Mr. Sledge, "seems to be helping our school. Not that we have fewer disciplinary problems, but that fewer trivial problems are sent to the office. I feel that our teachers have become more conscious of disciplinary techniques and of their responsibilities by having to use this referral."

It is important that parents and pupils know that they may review the disciplinary record at any mutually convenient time, that they may add statements to the record, and that the anecdotal referral forms will be removed from the record three years after the date of the referral.

Such a form can be used effectively at either the elementary or secondary level.

Assistant Principal Seldon Wood of Rocky Ford (Colorado) High School analyzes his discipline records periodically to determine the causes of referrals. Among his finds were these:

REFERRAL FORM FROM BROOKLYN PARK HIGH SCHOOL,

BALTIMORE, MARYLAND (IN TRIPLICATE)

REFERRAL AND FEED-BACK FORM

STUDENT _____ SECTION _____ TIME_____

TEACHER _____ DATE _____

NATURE OF PROBLEM _____

ACTION BEFORE REFERRAL
CONF. WITH PUPIL ____ Detention ____
Phone call home ____ Parent conf. ____
Letter to parents ____ Guid. conf. ____
OTHER ____

TEACHER/STUDENT/ADMINISTRATOR CONFERENCE
MY PLANNING PERIOD IS ____
STUDENT IS IN ROOM ____

ACTION BY ADMINISTRATION
DATE ____
Conf. with pupil (Warning/Reprimand) ____
detention ____
phone call to parents ____
formal letter (copy in your mailbox) ____
Conf with parent being requested ____
referred to Pupil Personnel Dept. ____
Suspension (until conf.) ____
Corporal punishment ____
OTHER ____

INITIALS ____

Figure 3-3

- A small number of teachers were referring a very high percentage of the students to the office.

- A high correlation existed between students with reading deficiencies and students with records of excessive truancy.

The records system had helped Mr. Wood in the identification of causes of discipline problems. Action was then taken to alleviate these causes by:

- Working with teachers, especially those responsible for a disproportionate number of referrals, so that they could improve their classroom management skills.

- Improving the reading program so that fewer pupils reached high school unable to do high school level work.

Mr. Wood has become one of the district's leading advocates for improving reading instruction throughout the district.

Some principals provide pupils with periodic opportunities to clear their records through demonstrating that they can control their own behavior. If, for example, a pupil, through conscientious effort, avoids being sent to the office for an entire semester, he might be invited into the principal's office for a "record-shredding" ceremony. Pupils enjoy participating in the destruction of negative information about them, and they feel a boost of morale knowing that their record is "clean."

3.02 Student Contracts

Another important tool in the management of discipline and attendance problems is the student contract. Such contracts are now widely used, both in elementary and secondary schools. They may, at times, involve one or more parents or even one or more peers who agree to help the student achieve his objectives.

Contracts, when completed successfully, form an important and positive part of the pupil's record.

Some contracts specify awards for the pupil as an additional stimulus to completing the agreement. Some even include penalties if the pupil fails to complete the contract. We urge caution in tying either rewards or penalties to contracts. It is sufficient reward for the pupil to see a positive addition to his discipline file. Pupils should enter into such agreements because they want to improve their behavior not because they want a special privilege.

A sample student contract form is shown in Figure 3–4.

Using such contracts, students have agreed to the following kinds of improvements in their behavior:

- be tardy to school no more than once in the next week
- stop fighting for two days
- do two nice things for his teacher during the next three days
- not be referred to the office by any teacher for the next two weeks
- dress and participate in P.E. activities every day for the next two weeks
- complete all math assignments on time for the next week

An important part of the contract is the part where various people can specify how they will help the pupils achieve their objec-

Student Contract

I, _____ , agree to accomplish the following:
1.   (pupil's name)

2.

3.

I, _____ , agree to assist the pupil in
        (administrator-teacher-parent)
the following way:
1.

2.

3.

This contract is effective from _____ until _____
                                    DATE   DATE
or until revised by mutual agreement.

SIGNATURES: _____   _____
                        Pupil   Parent

                    _____
                    Teacher or administrator

Figure 3-4

tives. A parent, for example, might agree to help a pupil get to school on time by agreeing to buy an alarm clock. A P.E. teacher may agree to encourage a pupil to participate in class regularly by agreeing to permit the pupil to work on an individualized project of special interest.

In writing a contract with a pupil, you should be careful not to expect too much. It is better to agree to easily achieved objectives at first. Once pupils experience success in controlling their own behavior, more complex contracts can be signed.

3.03 Improving Attendance

A recent survey of secondary principals, summarized in the *Nation's Schools Report* (9), revealed that the most "troublesome and frustrating" daily problems for principals are not discipline, vandalism, or money problems. Thirty-one percent of the principals responding to the survey listed "attendance problems, especially truancy" as their number one concern. Elementary principals will concur that attendance is a big headache.

Improving a school's attendance procedures is a big job requiring the participation of a number of people working for a long period of time. It is not a project that an administrator can accomplish over the summer vacation. It is best accomplished in most schools by a task force that has been given the responsibility of identifying the causes of attendance problems and then implementing solutions.

A school administrator should work closely with task force members so that they do not end up thinking up a lot of impractical tasks for him to accomplish. The responsibility of the task force should be spelled out before it begins work. Task force membership might include one or more parents, one or more teachers, one or more pupils, and a representative of the local police force. A sample charge to such a task force is reproduced in Figure 3–5.

**Sample Charge to a Task Force
for Improving Attendance**

The task force for improving attendance at the _____
School is charged with the following tasks:

1. Study the causes of attendance problems in the _____
School and report your findings to the principal by December 1, 19___.

2. Develop and recommend an action plan to improve attendance. The Action Plan should be designed to alleviate the causes of attendance problems which the study reveals. The action plan should define tasks and assign these tasks to individuals for completion.

3. Review the school's attendance policies and recommend revisions.

4. Review the school's absence reporting system and recommend revisions. Both segments of the system are to be studied.
   - the teacher-office-teacher reporting system.
   - the office-home-office reporting system

Figure 3–5

Following are some activities which the task force may wish to consider recommending:

(1) Arrange for local police officers to pick up truants on the street and in other public places and bring them to the school. Follow up this action with a phone call to parents and a letter to the parents confirming the call. This practice not only reduces truancy, it also reduces juvenile crime. Schools in Alexandria and Virginia Beach, Virginia, San Bernadino, California, and Lauderdale Lakes, Florida have reported highly successful programs.

(2) Improve supervision of halls, washrooms, and school grounds through employment of aides or monitors or through the use of parent volunteers. This improved supervision will cut down on single period cuts, a big problem in most secondary schools.

At Southeast High School in Ravenna, Ohio (800 pupils, 9–12), a matron is in the girls' washrooms at all times. The washrooms are no longer used as a dope drop, lounge, or lunchroom. Smoking has been stopped and single period absences have been reduced.

(3) Initiate a peer counseling program (children teach children) (6). In such programs volunteer pupils are trained by the school psychologist or by counselors to help other pupils.[1] Often, but not always, older pupils help younger ones. In the Palo Alto, California program (14) trained secondary pupils work with elementary pupils. They are trained by a group of psychologists, psychiatrists, and adult counselors in twelve weeks of after-school training sessions. Peer counseling not only improves attendance, it also improves the counselee's behavior generally and often improves his academic achievement.

At Littleton High School (Suburban Denver), one activity of the peer counseling program is the operation of an "attendance clinic." Littleton's principal, Melvin Harris, describes the program this way:

> Four administrators, two counselors and several peer counselors have volunteered to work with students in small groups, one day a week for nine week periods. Students are identified by the Assistant Principal as demonstrating poor school adjustment and may voluntarily participate in the Attendance Clinic or be assigned to attend as an alternative to suspension. These inter-action groups assist students in identifying problem causes, developing individual programs for dealing with non-attendance causes and encouraging each other to correct non-attendance patterns.

According to Mr. Harris, this program is off to a promising start.

---

[1] For more information on this concept, see Chapter 7, p. 162.

Attendance of many individuals has markedly improved and the number of groups is expanding.

(4) Initiate a group counseling program. Group counseling, like peer counseling, improves attendance by providing pupils with help in dealing with personal and learning problems. Participation in group counseling should be voluntary, and information divulged by pupils in such sessions must be considered confidential. Group counseling is most effective when it operates as an integral part of a school's pupil personnel services program.

(5) Call parents in the evening. Parents of pupils with attendance problems are often not available by telephone during the day. A secretary can make attendance calls in the evening, however, at minimal cost to the district. For this service the secretary may receive overtime pay or receive compensatory time off during the day.

(6) Hold individual and group counseling sessions in the evening.

(7) Eliminate or reduce half-day sessions. Your study of causes of attendance problems may show, as did the Norwich Free Academy study (11), that attendance is lower on days when the school operates less than a full day. Reducing the number of such days in your calendar may improve attendance.

(8) Develop more than one attendance policy for your school. Principal John Hoback of Boulder (Colorado) High School devised three different policies on attendance and asked parents to indicate which policy they wished to apply for their children.

● Policy 1 is a "He's on his own; don't bother me" policy designed for the highly responsible pupil who is trusted by his parents.

● Policy 2 is a "Just contact me if he's in trouble" policy. Most parents opted for this one.

● Policy 3 is the "Keep a close eye on him" policy, designed for parents who want their children supervised very closely.

Students' attendance files are tagged to indicate to the attendance office which policy is in effect for each pupil.

Figure 3–6 reproduces the registration form which Boulder parents can use to express their preference regarding these policies.

(9) Revise and streamline your reporting procedures. There may be unnecessary delays, inefficiencies, or bottle-necks in your reporting procedures. For example, some teachers may report absences inaccurately, results of teacher reports may be tabulated only once during the day, or you may not be spending enough time trying to contact hard-to-reach parents. Your task force's study of your procedures should identify ways to improve the efficiency of reporting.

BOULDER HIGH SCHOOL

Boulder, Colorado

BRING TO REGISTRATION

Dear Parent:

In order to help us work with you toward what is best for your son or daughter, we are attempting to individualize our attendance procedures. Please express to us which of the following procedures you would like for us to use with them regarding the reporting of absences. We will mark the records accordingly, notify each of their teachers of your desires, and do our best to follow through according to your wishes. If this form is not returned, we will follow Category 2.

*   *   *   *   *   *

CATEGORY 1—I feel that _____ should be completely responsible for his/her own attendance and for the consequences of any problem created. Please do **NOT** contact me about the problems other than severe illness, injury, or withdrawal from enrollment in school.

_____   _____
       Relationship   Signature

CATEGORY 2—I believe that _____ should handle most judgmental situations and negotiate solutions to most problems on his/her own without my involvement. Please contact me ONLY if his/her actions seem not to justify this. I wish to be notified ONLY when the conduct or attendance is creating a problem with him/her or for the smooth functioning of the class or of the school. This notification will occur BEFORE the problem becomes too serious to solve. I will notify the school of any circumstances beyond the student's control (such as illness or family emergency) which would prevent attendance.

_____   _____
       Relationship   Signature

CATEGORY 3—It is my belief that _____ should be present for every class on every day that is scheduled unless I have notified the

Figure 3-6

school otherwise. I want to be notified by school personnel as soon as is reasonable (usually the following day) after the absence or tardiness occurs.

_____	_____
Relationship	Signature
_____	_____
Home Phone	Business Phone

Other contact in case these fail   _____   _____

                                         Name   Phone

Figure 3–6 (cont'd.)

John Hoback, speaking at a recent convention of the National Association of Secondary School Principals (8), makes the following points regarding attendance:

1. The foundation of an effective attendance policy must be in the practices of the classroom teacher. Attendance symptoms are symptoms of a curriculum disease.[2]

2. Don't punish truancy by suspending a student from school. Such a practice is illogical and probably illegal.

3. Likewise other penalties such as reduction of grades or credit are in the long run less effective than the use of positive re-enforcement. Attendance problems will dwindle if courses are meaningful and if pupils are successful.

4. We need to expand out of the building opportunities for pupils to be successful in learning.

Mr. Hoback is challenging us to deal not only with the symptoms of attendance problems but also with causes; and he is implying that some of these causes lie within the nature of the school itself.

Your task force on attendance, then, may wish to study Chapters 5 through 8 of this book carefully. Thus, some of the task force's school improvement activities will be focused on improving the school's climate and its programs as well as its procedures.

---

[2] See Chapter 7 regarding ways to work on this "disease."

3.04 Start an In-School Suspension Program

Such programs are developed as an alternative to sending suspended pupils home. The purpose is to provide a means for removing disruptive students from the classroom and for providing such students with increased supervision, personal assistance with their studies and, in some cases, intensified counseling.

It is important that the program be seen primarily as a positive program designed to help students become successful in school. It is more than just a form of punishment. The in-school suspension room should be a reasonably pleasant place with competent, sensitive, positive teachers in charge. Pupils assigned to the room should know exactly what they must do to earn their way out.

In-school suspension programs are common in all parts of the country. One of the most extensive programs, however, operates in Dade County (Miami), Florida, where centers operate in all of the district's 50 junior and senior high schools. According to a recent report (3, p. 12–13) the program has resulted in a reduction of 10-day suspensions by 41 percent, 30-day suspensions by 70 percent, and expulsions by 83 percent. Activities in the centers include individual and group counseling, remedial work on reading and math, and trips to points of interest in the community. Most students return to their regular schedules after a couple of weeks in the center, and most are not suspended again.

Another program is reported by Robert L. Crane (5, p. 1–8), Principal of the Webber Junior High School in Saginaw, Michigan. At Webber disruptive pupils are excused from class to go to an "Adjusted Study" room for two, nonconsecutive days each week. In that room pupils work with a specialist and several volunteer tutors. The climate in the room might be described as "supportive" and "noncoercive." The program has helped pupils improve their overall grade averages and the number of referrals to the office for participating pupils has declined significantly.

The most comprehensive alternatives-to-suspension program we know of is the PASS (Positive Alternatives to Student Suspension) program, developed in Pinellas County (St. Petersburg), Florida. This program consists of eight interrelated components:

1. Staff development for a humanistic school
2. Humanistic activities in the regular classroom
3. Basic encounter for secondary students (group counseling)

4. Basic encounter for school personnel (including learning to "facilitate positive interaction")

5. Parent training groups (including "Parent Effectiveness Training")

6. The "Time-Out Room"

7. Students' School Survival Course

8. A Students' Home Survival Course

A complete description of this program, including a report on its effectiveness, is available from:

Pupil Personnel Services Demonstration Project
All Children's Hospital
801 6th Street South
St. Petersburg, Florida 33701

3.05 Establish an After School Behavior Clinic

This doesn't sound like a very creative idea; teachers and principals have been keeping pupils after school for at least four generations. What we are suggesting, however, is somewhat different from the traditional detention program, which is often more trouble than it is worth.

A behavior clinic is designed to help pupils control their own behavior. We would suggest that the program be instructional in nature and that it be coordinated with the school's counseling or social work services. Activities should be designed to help pupils understand their values and beliefs, their motivations, and their feelings about themselves, others, and their community.

One such clinic is operated by the East Baton Rouge Parish School District in Louisiana. In that district pupils are assigned to the clinic for minor offenses such as disobedience, smoking, or cutting class. If the offenses continue, the student is suspended.

3.06 Take Your Problem Students on a Retreat

Sometimes a group of staff members can make an impact on pupils with problems in a setting away from the regular school building. A retreat setting offers an environment which is relatively distraction-free and is conducive to opening communication among students and staff.

One such program, called the "Mt. Augustine Project" has been operating for several years in Parma, Ohio. Facilities for the retreat are provided by a convent near the high school—hence the project's title.

The project includes sophomores and juniors, 15 years of age and older, who have shown "functional, attitudinal, and academic deficiencies, and whose interests lie in vocational areas." The project consists of several week-long sessions, each session accommodating 25 pupils. Each session is staffed by:

- two teachers (one a vocational teacher)
- two administrators
- three counselors (one a vocational counselor)
- one youth counselor
- one psychologist
- one secretary

Activities include a wide variety of values clarification exercises (see Chapter 7), testing, and counseling activities. Mr. Wes Gaab, Principal of the Normandy High School, reports that the program, designed to reduce disruptive behavior, reduce drop-outs, and assist pupils make vocational choices, has been highly successful.

One girl, for example, had attempted suicide twice and was an in-school truant before she participated in the Mt. Augustine program. Describing this student this year, Mr. Gaab reports "she is a complete success story. She is a successful "C" student, has a new outlook on life, and is successfully involved in a vocational program and has not had one office report for the entire year. Her parents call it a miracle." Another student received "E's" for two years in most courses she attempted. Following participation in the program, she maintained her senior year on the honor roll. These stories, according to Mr. Gaab, are typical of many of the participants.

For further information about this program, see John Spinner's article in the *Guidance Clinic* (13).

3.07 Get Medical Help for Hyperactive Children

Some discipline problems have physical causes which can be remedied with appropriate treatment. A great deal has been written about the special problems of the "hyperkinetic child"—the child who is continuously distracted, has a short attention span, must always be moving. Such children often are inclined to fight, yell, run around the room. They are often irritable and hostile. The American Academy of Pediatrics has estimated that 3% of all elementary children may be diagnosed as hyperkinetic (10, p. 48). The Academy also estimates that 65% of such children can respond favorably to medication.

Discipline problems, then, can be reduced if proper medication can be administered on a regular basis to these children. The most commonly used drugs for such treatment are amphetamines and Ritalin.

We advise caution in the administering of such medication. It should, of course, be done only by doctor's prescription, with the consent of the pupil and his parents, and under the supervision of the school nurse.[3] Other alternatives for improving the child's behavior should be explored before a program of medication is chosen.

The "judicious" use of drugs to help control pupil behavior has been endorsed by a study team of the Department of Health, Education and Welfare and by the American Academy of Pediatrics (10, p. 49-52).

3.08 Develop a Referral-Type Behavior Modification Program

Behavior modification may be defined as a technique for improving pupil behavior through the use of B. F. Skinner's principles of operant conditioning. Briefly, the system has the following characteristics:

1) The teacher rewards good behavior and ignores disruptive behavior. Often a system of rewards such as tokens which can be exchanged for privileges is used.

2) Specific behavioral objectives are defined, and the pupil is rewarded for achieving the objectives.

3) Personal praise is gradually substituted for token rewards as the pupil gains more control over his own behavior. At an appropriate stage the tokens are phased out.

4) Isolation areas are designated where pupils who have lost control of their emotions can take "time out" to regain control.

---

[3]In Taft, California parents have sued the schools for $500,000, alleging that drugs were administered to children on the basis of insufficient physical examinations and that parents were coerced into giving their permission.

5) Pupils gradually learn to be motivated more by their success in learning and less by their desire for artificial rewards or by their desire to please the teacher.

Initially these techniques were used only on adult mental patients suffering from severe psychoses. Now they are widely used in classrooms containing, for the most part, normal children.

We do not advocate the widespread use of behavior modification in the usual classroom or laboratory setting. Such techniques tend to teach pupils to learn for the wrong reasons, tend to make learning superficial, and are inconsistent with democratic principles of classroom management (4). Critics often accuse teachers of using the system to foster dependency rather than independence. Critics have also likened the "time out" rooms to closets in which pupils are locked for being bad.

Regardless of the criticisms, however, behavior modification works. It is a system which, when used by well-trained, sensitive, caring teachers, can teach pupils who have severe behavioral problems to control their own behavior.

Some guidelines for implementing such a program in your school district:

1) It should operate only as a referral program for pupils who have severe behavioral problems.

2) Referral should be made through a fully certified psychologist and with parental consent.

3) The teachers should be specially trained to operate the program.

4) The instructional area should be a part of a school but somewhat isolated from other instructional areas.

5) Space allocated should be ample and the area should be specially designed for the program. Group size should be very small (six is a large group).

6) Follow-up, reentry services should be provided for each pupil as he begins to return to a regular classroom environment.

Such a program is appropriate only for a small number of pupils. It should not develop into a general "dumping ground" program.

One such classroom, in the Wiley School in Urbana, Illinois, operates as a part of the district's special education program. Six months in the program is usually sufficient to enable the pupil to return to regular classroom instruction. The program is of benefit to from twelve to fifteen elementary pupils per year who, without the program, would be making life miserable for themselves, their classmates, and their teachers.

Urbana's special education teacher, Lynn Hoffmann, reports that only 10% of the pupils who have been through her program require special help in adjusting to normal classroom routines.

3.09 Doing Something About Smoking

"The smoking dilemma," says one secondary school principal (7), "is an exercise in contradiction, hypocrisy, and joylessness." We couldn't agree more.

Yet there is a need in most schools to resolve the smoking issue as a part of the general shaping up of the school process. There are, of course, problems:

1) In many states it is illegal for persons under 18 to smoke. If a school establishes smoking areas for pupils it can be accused of encouraging lawlessness.

2) Custom permits adult smoking in school offices and faculty lounges. Thus schools not permitting student smoking can be accused of operating under a double standard.

3) School rules prohibiting smoking on school property are virtually unenforceable. Even if teachers, administrators, and the nonacademic staff together make a strong effort to eliminate student smoking, the results will be disappointing and temporary.

4) There is now little question that cigarette smoking is harmful to a person's health. Schools, then, which establish smoking areas can be accused of fostering unhealthful attitudes among youth.

5) Instructional programs which highlight the harmful effects of tobacco have, like drug education programs, been notoriously unsuccessful in discouraging pupils and staff from smoking.

Resolving the smoking issue in your school, then, will not be easy.

We recommend, however, that you consider the following actions:

1) Include in your school's student code a statement that it is the school's position that the use of tobacco is harmful to

health and that the staff of the school will do everything possible to discourage smoking among staff members and students.

2) Organize units of instruction on the harmful effects of tobacco. Report to parents where those units are located in the curriculum and what the objectives of the unit are.

3) Enforce a policy of no smoking when adults use the building at night.

4) Offer a "stop smoking" clinic for students and interested staff.

5) Display anti-smoking posters and hold seminars on the smoking dilemma.

THEN, after you have done these things,

6) Designate one or more outside areas as smoking areas. Develop, with student cooperation, a set of rules for the area.

Mr. Eugene Cave, Principal of Flood Junior High in Englewood, Colorado, involved students, parents, counselors, teachers, and police officials in an extensive problem solving effort. He then sent a letter describing the newly developed policy to all parents. This letter is reproduced in Figure 3–7. Similar information was given to each student in memorandum form.

MARY LOUISE FLOOD JUNIOR HIGH SCHOOL
Englewood, Colorado

Dear Parent,

At the request of some students and parents, we at Flood Junior High are making an attempt to meet the desires of a few. We recognize that some of our students smoke, furthermore we have been informed that this is with your full approval. We do not wish to punish a student who smokes, and does so honestly within the limits of school rules and policies.

We want it to be well known that we *do not* believe that smoking is in the best interest of your child's health. However, we are placing this responsibility with you and your child. We can no longer risk a fire in the building due to smoking in an unauthorized area, nor do we choose to play games by turning our heads.

At present students are permitted to smoke on the southwest corner of

Figure 3-7

Kenyon and Lincoln before and after school only. Students have also been "permitted" to smoke at noon—but this has never been an announced policy.

If you sign this letter your son/daughter will be permitted to smoke at noon on the Lincoln/Kenyon corner *only* with the following provisions.

A. No smoking will be permitted in any other area of the school. Students smoking outside that area will be subject to three or five day suspensions from school. With a required parent conference for reinstatement.

B. Students must have the bottom portion of this letter stating that parents approved on file in our office.

C. Students will be allowed a reasonable time to have their cigarette (not to exceed ten minutes) and then must return to the grounds.

D. Students entering the area will be responsible for cleaning the area.

E. If the above regulations are not met the privilege will be revoked.

Should you have questions regarding this information, please contact us at school.

Sincerely,

Eugene Cave
Principal

Steven Cohen
Assistant Principal

I approve of my student's smoking at noon and pledge my support of the above regulations.

Student Signature	Date	Parent Signature	Date

Address	Work Phone	Home Phone

Figure 3-7 (cont'd.)

The result, according to Mr. Cave, is that smoking has been eliminated in washrooms and vandalism has been reduced. The policy is supported by parents and students.

The most frequently reported problems with outside smoking areas are the difficulty of keeping the areas clean and the difficulty in obtaining parental support for the policy.

Mr. Cave solved the first problem by assigning an aide to supervise the area. He solved the second by extensively involving parents in the setting of the policy.

The Flood Junior High School solution may not be appropriate for all schools. It is, however, a solution which is gaining increased acceptance.

3.10 Handle Discipline Problems Legally

If you are a practicing, front-line administrator dealing with lots of people, the chances are you will eventually find yourself in court— at least once. If you haven't had a school law course for a few years, maybe you should spend some time reviewing the implications of several recent legal decisions dealing with discipline. Likewise, if you are not thoroughly familiar with your state's school code regarding discipline, perhaps you should review its contents.

Following is a very brief summary of eight legal issues now restricting the actions of school officials. As you go about the day-to-day task of administering discipline in your school you should be thoroughly familiar with these issues. The court cases referred to are summarized in Figure 3–8.

Glossary of Famous Legal Decisions

Baker vs. Owen 395 F Supp. 294 (1975). The decision supports the use of corporal punishment but stated that the child has a right to due process.

Brown vs. Board of Education of Topeka, 347, U.S. 483 (Kan. 1954), established that education is a right which must be made available to all on equal terms.

Goss vs. Lopez (95 S. Ct. 729 Ohio 1975). A Supreme Court decision which established in 1975 that school officials cannot tarnish a person's reputation or deprive him from attending school without a "fair hearing."

Figure 3–8

Ingraham vs. Wright (U.S. Court of Appeals, 5th Circuit, 525 F 2d 909)
    1976. This court disagreed with the *Baker vs. Owen* decision by ruling
    that due process steps (notice of hearing, etc.) need not be followed
    in dispensing corporal punishment.

Johnson vs. Paulsboro N.S. (Civil Action No. 172-70, D.C. N.J. April 14,
    1970). Established the right of married students to participate in
    extra-curricular activities.

Overton vs. New York 20 N.Y. 2nd 260, 229 N. E. 2nd 283 N.Y. 2nd 22
    (1967) 39 V.S.L.W. 3322 (1971). Established an administrator's right
    and duty to inspect a pupil's locker if reasonable grounds exist.

Perry vs. Granada School District (300 F Supp. 748) Mississippi 1969.
    This decision established the right of unwed mothers to attend school
    unless it could be shown that they are grossly lacking in moral
    character.

Schmidt vs. Mt. Vernon, Civil Action #2246 (D.C. Missouri, September 29,
    1971). Established the right of a pregnant student to an education
    equal to that given other members of her class.

State of Delaware vs. Baccino 282A, 2nd 869 (1971). This decision reaf-
    firmed that the principal stands *in loco parentis* insofar as personal
    searches are concerned. Evidence obtained by an assistant principal
    who searched a student's coat was declared admissible in court.

State vs. Stein (203) Kan. 638, 456 P. 2nd 1 (1969), cert. denied 90 S. Ct.
    996 (1970). This is a famous case which established (1) that it is
    proper for school officials to inspect student lockers to prevent their
    illegal use, (2) the *Miranda* warning ("you have the right to remain
    silent," etc.) does not have to be given prior to a search, and (3) that
    the student does not have "exclusive" ownership of his locker insofar
    as school authorities are concerned.

Tinker vs. Des Moines (393 U.S. 503) 1969. This is the famous "black
    armband" case in which students peacefully protesting the Vietnam
    War were suspended. The Supreme Court ruled, in effect, that students
    do not "shed their constitutional rights at the schoolhouse gate."
    Ruling means that where a conflict exists between individual rights
    and school regulations, the regulations will be supported only if they
    are essential to the orderly functioning of the school.

Figure 3–8 (cont'd.)

1. Due Process

Briefly, due process means that an individual accused of a serious
violation of school rules has the right:

- to know the charges against him
- to hear evidence and submit evidence on his own behalf
- to show that the rule in question is unreasonable, arbitrary, capricious, discriminatory, or too vague to be understood

2. Corporal Punishment

Corporal punishment in schools is illegal in some states. In others, the courts have held that corporal punishment is legal so long as it is not unreasonable and excessive. It is unclear, however, whether an administrator can administer corporal punishment if parents object and refuse to administer the punishment themselves. It is also unclear whether due process must be followed in administering corporal punishment. An administrator may be held criminally liable if the punishment is held to be unreasonable or excessive.

We are opposed to corporal punishment both on practical and philosophical grounds. It is, we believe, inconsistent for a principal who hits kids to ask them to stop hitting one another. Furthermore, we seriously doubt the effectiveness of corporal punishment as a means of helping pupils modify their behavior.

We realize, however, that you may not agree with this point of view. So if you feel that you must use corporal punishment, we suggest the following procedure:

- Be sure that the student has been warned at least once that the specific action he is being punished for would result in corporal punishment.
- Be prepared to document the fact that other means of punishment have been used and that corporal punishment is a "last resort."
- Notify the parent that you are going to administer corporal punishment.
- Administer corporal punishment against the wishes of the parent only if you are willing to accept the risk of being sued.
- Administer the punishment in the presence of an adult witness.

Consult your state's school code for information on what your state laws require. State laws vary considerably on this topic.

3. Searching Students and Their Property

Recent decisions indicate that school officials may search a pupil's locker when there is reasonable grounds for such a search. This may be done without a warrant and without the student's permission. If, however, your purpose in searching the locker is to obtain incriminating evidence which may be used in court, you should invite a police officer with a warrant to join you in the search.

Searching a student's person is risky business unless you can show "probable cause," i.e., information which indicates a strong likelihood that the student is carrying harmful or dangerous articles or substances.

Some suggestions regarding searching a student, his property, or his locker:

- School policies should clearly state that lockers and students themselves are liable to search if, in the opinion of the administration, such search is necessary for the protection of other students and for maintenance of an orderly school environment.
- The student should be present when the property or locker search is conducted.
- An adult witness to the search should also be present.
- General, 100% locker searches, in the absence of a bomb threat or a massive drug problem, are not advised.
- If a student is found to be in possession of illegal materials, the parent should be called first, then the police.

4. Suspension

It is generally agreed that you can't suspend a student from school without minimal due process, consisting of at least the following:

- The student should be given oral or written notice of the charges.
- If he denies the charges he should be informed of the nature of the evidence against him and given an opportunity to present his side of the story.
- There need be no delay between when notice is given and the time of the hearing.

It is not necessary to allow a student to obtain counsel, to call witnesses on his own behalf, or to cross-examine witnesses.

In case a student's presence in school constitutes a continuing danger to persons or property or an ongoing threat of disrupting the academic process, he may be immediately removed from school. Notice and a hearing, however, must be provided within 72 hours after the removal.

Be sure that whoever conducts the hearing cannot be accused of having prejudged the case.

5. Expulsion

Each state's school code stipulates different procedures for expelling students. Prior to initiating expulsion proceedings you should consult your school attorney. In general, expulsions require that a student's parents receive written notice of the offense, that a formal hearing be held, that the pupil be informed of his right of representation by counsel, and that a written record be made of the decision.

Expulsions must be handled with fidelity to all legal requirements. Board members and other school officials may be held liable for damages if they participate in any action deemed to violate a student's constitutional rights.

6. Personal Appearance

Most court cases regarding the personal appearance of students have dealt with the right of school authorities to regulate hair styles. The Supreme Court, as yet, has refused to hear such cases and federal district courts have not ruled consistently. Therefore, according to one attorney, "the right to wear long hair depends on where a student goes to school" (10, p. 20). Hair regulations, according to *Discipline Crisis in the Schools,* have been sustained in Colorado, Texas, Kansas, New Mexico, California, in the South, and in the Michigan-Ohio corridor. In contrast, federal courts have rules that regulations on hair styles are invalid in Minnesota, Iowa, Virginia, Maine, Wisconsin, some Midwestern States, and Pennsylvania.

In general, you can be on firm ground in regarding pupil appearance only if your regulations prohibit student hair styles or manner of dress which present a clear and present danger to the student's health and safety, cause an interference with work, create classroom or school disorder, or damage school property.

In devising regulations on personal appearance you should be careful not to violate the intent of Title IX sexual discrimination regulations within the Civil Rights Act. One school district in Colorado is currently in trouble with the U.S. Civil Rights Office because of a school regulation which permits boys to wear jeans but prohibits girls from doing the same. The rule also regulates the length of boys' hair without also regulating the length of girls' hair.

While all of this may seem pretty ridiculous or even humorous on the surface, there is nothing funny about being dragged into court for trying to regulate hair styles or student dress. If you haven't reviewed your own policies with your attorney recently, maybe you should do so.

7. Civil Rights

School officials these days are constantly being accused of violating the civil rights of students and staff. Each time you make a decision to punish a pupil you are opening yourself up to possible charges of unlawful discrimination on the basis of sex, race, religion, or marital status.

School systems and schools are frequently charged with racial discrimination if they suspend or expel a higher percentage of one racial group than another. The best protection against such accusations is a good record system which shows that due process has been followed in all suspension and expulsion cases. It also helps to involve civil rights leaders in developing your regulations and procedures so that they see you as a fair-minded person who is not out to discriminate against any particular racial group. Frequently, also, such leaders can be of great assistance in influencing young people in their neighborhood who are discipline problems. Try to make friends with your community civil rights leaders; you need all the friends you can get.

Much legal action recently has centered around questions of sex discrimination. "In general," says Robert Acherly (2) "there are now very few circumstances in which distinctions between school pupils on the basis of sex or marital status will be sustained by the courts." For example:

- You can't exclude a female pupil from school just because she gets pregnant. Whether she's married or not, she still has a right to an education equal to that being received by others in her class.

- Married students have the right to participate in extra-curricular activities.

- Female students, generally, cannot be excluded on the basis of sex from participating in all male teams in so-called "non-contact sports," especially if competition in that sport on an all female team is not available. Whether or not they can be excluded from participating on male teams engaged in contact sports is not clear.

Obviously, if you have not already done so, you need to study carefully the implications of Title IX of the Federal Education Act of 1972 on your school's policies and regulations. Also, you might form a task force to recommend revisions to existing practices. You are required by Title IX to adopt a student grievance procedure. A good "model," developed in Glendale, Arizona, is printed in a recent *Nations Schools Report* (12, p. 5).

The National Association of Secondary Schools Publication, *A Legal Memorandum,* of June, 1975 (1, p. 7) offers the following suggestions for avoiding financial liability under the Civil Rights Act of 1971:

- Make and enforce any rule which appears to abridge civil rights only after careful consideration. If at all possible get the advice of counsel.

- If a rule or its enforcement appears to abridge a pupil's civil rights, be certain that it is necessary, reasonably related to the school's purposes and administered without discrimination.

- Set up fundamentally fair . . . procedures . . . for suspension and expulsion.

- Make a reasonable attempt to keep up with court decisions governing student conduct in your jursidiction.

8. School Newspapers

In general, the courts have tended to support students' rights to publish newspapers, free of censorship, which express unpopular views. Teachers and administrators can exercise some "perfectly legal safeguards" and "one of them is to view a publication before it is distributed to make sure it is not so inflammatory that it would clearly disrupt the school."

The principal has the right and obligation to regulate the time and place of distribution of publications. According to *Discipline Crisis in the Schools* (10, p. 21) he may legally ban publications from the school in order to:

- Prevent incitement of others to commit unlawful acts.

- Prevent inflammatory words that would lead to physical retaliation, such as gang warfare.

- Protect the sensibilities of others against such things as racial and ethnic slurs, slander, libel, and obscenities.
- Prevent overt disrespect for the American flag.

The following advice, given by Robert Akerly in *The Reasonable Exercise of Authority* (2, p. 11) should apply:

> School sponsored publications should be free from policy restrictions outside of the normal rules for responsible journalism. These publications should be as free as other newspapers in the community to report the news and to editorialize . . .

> Non-school-sponsored papers and other publications, including an "underground press" should not be prohibited, assuming they, too, observe the normal rules for responsible journalism.

These eight legal issues are important. The extent to which you understand them may to a large extent determine how much time you spend in court and how large a fee your district's lawyer will earn.

In writing this section, we have relied heavily on three sources. We recommend that you study these sources carefully and that you begin a resource file on legal decisions which affect your authority as a school administrator. The three publications, annotated in the bibliography, are:

Discipline Crisis in Schools, a publication of the National School Public Relations Association, pp. 13–22 (10).

The Reasonable Exercise of Authority II, a publication of the National Association of Secondary School Principals, (2).

A series of papers entitled *A Legal Memorandum,* published periodically by the National Association of Secondary School Principals (1).

Chapters 2 and 3 have dealt with a variety of ways school administrators, with help from students, staff, and parents, can shape up a school. The latter part of Chapter 3 provides a number of suggestions for doing all of this legally, with due regard for student's rights.

A humane learning environment is not necessarily a sloppy one. Schools, if they are to serve the needs of all of their students, must be orderly places in which the principles of justice common in our society as a whole prevail. A school can be orderly without being oppressive.

Shaping Up the School III—
Helping Teachers Reduce
Discipline Problems

4

Little can be done to reduce discipline problems in a school without the active involvement of teachers. Many discipline problems originate in classes which are managed by teachers. With help, teachers can reduce the number of these problems markedly. Other discipline problems originate outside the classroom—in hallways, cafeterias, on the playground, and at athletic and social events. Teachers can assume key responsibility for doing something about these problems too. A key organizational unit for solving nonclassroom discipline problems is the task force—a group of individuals working together to solve problems and manage their solutions.

The first nine suggestions in this chapter define ways the administrator can help teachers reduce discipline problems in the classroom. The tenth suggestion defines how the administrator can help teachers assume leadership in reducing discipline problems elsewhere.

We admit at the beginning that this chapter is biased in favor of what might be described as a humane, student-centered approach which operates within previously defined limits. Our suggestions are based on the following five assumptions:

1) Positive, productive behavior, both in and out of the classroom, is dependent, to a large extent, on people's self-esteem. People need to feel that they are "OK" and that others are "OK" too. They need to believe that they can succeed in the tasks set before them.

2) Our behavior is governed principally by our basic needs—especially our need for physical survival (food, liquid, shelter, sex, sleep, and oxygen), safety, belonging, love, esteem, growth and development (self-actualization), curiosity, and beauty.

These basic needs are interdependent to the extent that denial of any one of the needs affects the person's ability to achieve any of the others.

It follows then that a classroom and a school must be managed in such a way that these basic needs are met. A pupil coming to school hungry, for example, will learn little of value until he is fed.

Once basic needs are met, many discipline problems evaporate.

3) Teacher behavior most likely to result in high productivity and a low level of discipline problems has been defined. School administrators can help teachers improve their own behavior so that discipline problems both in and out of the classroom are reduced.

4) The behavior modification approach is rejected for general classroom use for reasons already detailed in Chapter 3. (See Chapter 3, p 70.) Manipulation of children in a synthetic environment should be replaced with openness, authenticity, and caring.

5) We assume that teachers can and will be willing to assume responsibility in working with pupils, parents, and administrators in eliminating the causes of discipline problems wherever they occur, in or out of the classroom. A promising organizational device for helping teachers do this is the task force.

These five assumptions underlie all ten of the suggestions which follow.

4.01 Identify Teachers Who Need Help

It is difficult to help teachers who are having discipline problems unless you know who they are. You have, of course, a number of informal ways to identify such teachers. Pupils will tell you about them and so will other teachers, if you have their confidence. You can identify others through classroom observations. Some will come to you on their own because they want your help.

One useful technique, in addition to the above, for identifying teachers with special problems, is the referral analysis. Assuming that you have in operation an efficient record-keeping system such as described in Chapter 3, you might proceed with the following steps:

1) Ask the secretary in the discipline office (or the principal's office) to keep a log of all referrals by each teacher. This log might resemble a financial ledger or it might be kept on index cards.

2) For each referral the secretary should list the following information:
   - Date and time
   - Pupil's name
   - Referring teacher's name
   - Reason for referral

She would obtain this information from the regular referral form sent to the office by the teacher (see Figure 3–1, p. 57).

3) Periodically (one or twice a month) the secretary will prepare a summary of teacher referrals.

Such a summary can provide the administrator with what amounts to an early warning system that something may be wrong in a particular teacher's class.

It is not unusual for such analyses to reveal that as many as 2/3 of the school's referrals are originating with only 1/10th of the teachers. Chances are these teachers need help.

If you concentrate your time and effort on those teachers who need your help most, you have a good chance of reducing the overall number of referrals in a short period of time.

A word of caution. One principal we know initiated a system similar to that just described, then made the statement, "Now, we're going to find out who the bad teachers are." As you might predict, his faculty immediately declared war on his project. In implementing this idea, be careful not to offend the teachers you are trying to help.

4.02 Visit Classes

It is almost impossible to help teachers if you don't know what is going on in their classrooms. It is essential that you spend as much time as possible out in the classrooms teaching, observing, helping individual pupils, asking questions, making suggestions, and, in general, making yourself useful. You can, of course, help with individual problem students by counseling with them, arranging for parent-teacher-pupil conferences, obtaining psychological or medical services, or arranging for special programs. You can often be much more helpful to a potentially disruptive student if you work with him before he's referred to you rather than afterwards.

It is important that teachers and pupils view you as a capable teacher. When an opportunity arises to demonstrate some creative teaching, take it. You will earn respect and credibility that way.

It should, of course, be clear that your purpose in the classroom is not to evaluate teachers. Rather it is to help them do a better job with their pupils. Formal evaluation visits are different kinds of visits.

You will no doubt spend more time with those teachers who need your help most. New teachers, especially, need the reassurance of knowing that an administrator is readily available and willing to help. Your goal in spending time in classrooms is that you be viewed eventually by teachers as a participant, not as a visitor.

Your presence in planning sessions with teachers is also important. If you have demonstrated that you know what you are talking about, teachers will welcome your suggestions for making their classrooms more productive and exciting.

You can't improve discipline in your school by staying in your office. It is essential that you spend your time where the action is.

4.03 Become Acquainted with the Literature on the Subject of Discipline and Motivation

The "References and Bibliography" section of this book is annotated so that you can choose books and articles which will help you help teachers. We especially recommend that you review all of the references for this chapter so that you will be acquainted with some of the latest instruments and techniques regarding the improvement of discipline. Some of the references cited for other chapters may also be valuable.

You can provide leadership for your school only if you have knowledge of what is likely to work and what is not likely to work for teachers desiring to improve pupil behavior and morals.

4.04 Start a Classroom Discipline Reference Center

The materials described in the "References and Bibliography" section of this chapter can serve as basic materials in your school's

"Improvement of Discipline" reference center. Additional materials can be donated by staff members, parents, and pupils.

The reference center would be used by task forces working on improving discipline in the school, by staff members participating in the school's inservice education program, and by individual teachers seeking to improve discipline in their own classes. Many principals locate such a reference center in or near their offices.

Much time can be wasted by people trying to shape up a school if they do not know what they are doing. A well-stocked, well-used reference center will provide you with insurance against well-intentioned, uninformed tinkering.

4.05 Implement a Continuous Inservice Education Program

All staff, not just teachers, should participate in inservice programs. Such programs, when combined with individual support for teachers having difficulty, can make a big difference in the number of discipline problems in a school.

As a result of one comprehensive program, the faculty of the Marcus Elementary School in Dallas (6) achieved the following in only one year:

- Reduced the number of referrals to the office by over 50%
- Reduced absentees by 15%
- Produced significant pupil achievement gains in reading, language, and work study skills

The Marcus School inservice program was designed around the 15 regularly scheduled staff development sessions provided by the district's calendar. The sessions were led by the principal, who was assisted by resource persons from the Dallas Independent School District, from a local medical school, and from a nearby university. This program was unique in four ways:

1) Teachers implemented the classroom management principles they learned in the 15 sessions. Each teacher concentrated his efforts on meeting the needs of only three "experimental" pupils in his classroom. These three pupils were matched with three control group pupils who were unknown to the teacher.

2) Appropriate instruments were used. For example, an interaction analysis system was administered in a pre and post

survey by an outside observer. Thus teachers could document their progress in providing rewarding experiences for pupils.

3) As a result of the inservice sessions specific changes were made in the way the school as a whole operated. A number of "disciplinary alternatives" were identified and put into effect, among them:

  - stepped up school-sponsored activities

  - group guidance sessions

  - increased tutorial efforts

  - student affairs committee assistance with student problems

  - principal and teachers eating lunch with troubled students

  - informal "getting to know you" conferences between teachers and pupils.

4) The evaluation of each teacher's growth in classroom management skills was done by that teacher himself. Self-evaluation was chosen over the use of an outside evaluator because self-evaluation is comparatively nonthreatening. It was also felt that teachers would gain more insight into their own behavior if they used self-evaluation.

Inservice programs, then, to be successful must be action programs. Staff members become highly motivated to improve themselves when they see that they can use their improved competence to improve the school in several specific ways. Self-improvement is seen as being essential to school improvement.

Following are some suggested topics you may wish to schedule for your inservice sessions:

  - How this inservice program will improve the school. How to link self-improvement to school improvement

  - Action planning for teachers. How to develop a plan for classroom climate improvement

  - Instruments you can use to measure classroom climate and your own and your pupils' behavior (Use university consultants for these sessions) (3) (10) (12)

  - How to identify individual pupil learning styles and needs

  - How to design learning experiences appropriate to various

learning styles (e.g., active learning experiences, creative learning experiences)

- How to use Glasser's "Schools Without Failure" techniques and tools in the classroom[1] (several sessions) (4)
- How to implement the "Theory of Logical Consequences" (2) as a way of promoting self-discipline
- Transactional analysis as a way of improving self-esteem[2]
- How to implement Karen Todd's ideas for promoting mental health in the classroom (13)
- How to implement Rolf Muuss' concept of "First Aid in Social Situations" (7)
- Providing for basic needs in the classroom. Applying Maslow's psychology to improving discipline and morale (5)
- Managing the "Magic Circle"—the Human Development Program approach to preventive mental health (9)
- How to work on a task force. How to solve problems systematically

The main purpose of the large group meetings of such an inservice program is to acquaint the staff with the latest thinking of experts in the field of motivation and behavior, to teach them how to use the instruments necessary to diagnose their situation and to measure their progress, and to provide them with planning skills so that they know how to develop an action plan to improve pupil behavior.

A number of very useful suggestions for inservice activities can be found in Read and Simon's *Humanistic Education Sourcebook* (10) and Schmuck's *A Humanistic Psychology of Education* (12).

4.06 As a Part of Your Inservice Program Provide Your Teachers with Diagnostic Instruments and Teach Them How to Use Them

Many excellent diagnostic instruments are available. Some are described in the books recommended in the "References and Bibliography" section of this book. Others can be suggested by specialists at your State University or nearby college of education.

---

[1] Information regarding printed materials, films, instruments, and consultant help can be obtained from *Learning,* 530 University Avenue, Palo Alto, CA 94301.

[2] See reference to Thomas Harris, Chapter 7, #6.

Generally, these instruments are of three types:

- Instruments to define the quality of the learning environment
- Instruments to describe teacher behavior in the classroom
- Instruments which describe teacher-pupil and pupil-pupil interaction patterns

We are including, in Appendix C, an instrument of our own design which teachers may use to describe their own perceptions of their behavior in the classroom.

This instrument can be used by the teacher, with the help of the principal, a consultant, or a colleague, to identify where the biggest gaps are between "what is" and "what ought to be." Where those gaps exist, the teacher can plan self-improvement activities.

4.07 Teach Your Staff How to Plan for School Improvement and Self Improvement

Once a teacher has identified ways he would like to improve his own competencies and his own classroom situation, he is ready to initiate a self-improvement plan.

One very popular planning format used widely by both teachers and administrators is the Self Performance Achievement Record (SPAR) (8), reproduced in Figure 4-1.

This instrument, on one sheet of paper, summarizes the individual's plans for self-improvement and for improvement of the classroom situation. The teacher is then asked to make a list of what would be considered as "evidences of success." This list describes the conditions which would exist if the individual's objectives are achieved. For example:

Objective:	*Evidence of Success:*
1) Pupils in my classroom will grow in self-esteem	1a) The number of fights on the playground and in the classroom will be reduced.
	1b) Tardiness and absenteeism will be reduced.
	1c) Pupils will smile more and argue less in my classroom.

Teachers and administrators should read the complete manual of instructions prior to using SPAR (8). It is not a difficult instrument to use but it has limited usefulness if it is not used properly.

SELF PERFORMANCE ACHIEVEMENT RECORD (SPAR)

I What is your institutional
or personal GOAL Statement?
(See pages 5–7*)

_____

_____

_____

Name _____

Date _____

Based on the total improvement
needs of your school or yourself, this project represents———

_____ a high priority need.

_____ a low priority need.

II What are the ACTIVITIES? (See pages 7–9)	**III** What are the OBJECTIVES? (See pages 9–20)	**IV** What are the EVIDENCES OF SUCCESS? (See pages 20–24)

*Page numbers refer to sections of the *Self Performance Achievement Record.* A CFK Ltd. Occasional Paper.

Figure 4–1

V INDIVIDUALIZED CONTINUING EDUCATION PROGRAM (See pages 24–26) What new abilities do *you* need to achieve this project?		VI What are the STARTING AND COMPLETION DATES? (See page 26)	VII LOG OF PROGRESS REPORTS (See pages 26–27)
What new skills, attitudes, or knowledge do you need?	How will you obtain each new need?		

Figure 4-1 (cont'd.)

In most schools where SPAR is used, administrators used the instrument first for their own planning, then gradually introduced the process to teachers.

Less complicated formats for teachers can be devised. Figure 4-2 shows a simple four-column format developed by Mrs. Amelia Valdez, a junior high school teacher in Alamosa, Colorado. She has used this format to list several activities designed to improve the behavior of potential dropouts. Mrs. Valdez's plan does not include self-improvement activities, but such activities can be identified when her plan is revised the first time.

Another format, developed by the Denver Public Schools, is reproduced in Figure 4-3.

Whatever format is used, teachers should be encouraged to identify ways to improve both themselves and their classrooms.

4.08 Publish Guidelines of Lists of Suggestions for Teachers and Parents

Scores of articles have been written listing "Dos and Don'ts" for parents and teachers who want to improve discipline. One excellent set, for example, was published by psychologist Thomas Banville in *The Instructor* (1), another is offered in *Discipline Crisis in Schools* (see Chapter 3, #10).

Such statements are valuable to teachers because they express in concrete form the philosophy of a school. You can tell a lot about a school by reading such statements. You won't always like what you read.

One document we examined, for example, contained the following pieces of advice under the label "Hints for Discipline."[3]

- "While any dictionary will give several definitions of the word "discipline," we will use the term to mean "training to act in accordance with established rules.""

- "It is wise to be wary of pupil-teacher planning when the rules are to be established at the start of the semester. . . . It is unnecessarily risky to allow the class to set rules of behavior."

- "Act tough the first, and possibly the second day . . . . Students must understand that this teacher knows his business and that they will have to toe the mark . . . . Act stern, unyielding,

---

[3]Some phrasing has been edited for the purpose of brevity.

A PLAN FOR IMPROVING NEGATIVE STUDENT BEHAVIOR*

OVERALL GOAL: To recycle or change the behavior of the potential dropout students from negative to positive, achieving, successful behavior.

Objectives-Outcomes	Evaluation	Processes	Budget
1. The learner will know how to get help.	1. Checklist of attitudes and needs assessment.	1. Class Discussions concerning acceptable behavior.	No Money is Needed!
2. The learner will want to achieve.	2. Achievement tests.	2. Brainstorming on kinds of acceptable behavior.	All materials are already available or teacher and student can provide when needed.
3. The learner will experience success.	3. Conference with student and plan.	3. Role playing.	
4. Language skills will be expanded.	4. Discuss plans with staff.	4. Teacher involvement with students.	
5. The learner will develop his own talents—Creativity.	5. Conferences with peer group and parents.	5. Students may work in small group or with a partner.	
	6. Later on in the school year Checklist of attitudes to evaluate behavior from negative to positive.	6. Plan activities for success and praise successful achievement.	
	7. Achievement tests for achievement growth.	7. Teacher keeps a log.	
	8. Teacher Observation.	8. Student keeps notebook of successful Language Arts work.	

*Reproduced with the permission of Mrs. Amelia Valdez.

Figure 4-2

94

DENVER PUBLIC SCHOOLS

Division of Education

MBO/R PLAN

OVERALL GOAL:

Year _____

Objectives-Outcomes	Evaluation	Processes	Budget

Figure 4-3

and sure of yourselves in your first appearance before the class."

- "An assigned seating plan is an important part of establishing of routines and preventative discipline."

- "In any of our activities or discussions students will be expected to participate. They must understand that in order to be recognized they must raise their hands and wait to be called on by the teacher or student-chairman (if there is a panel discussion in progress)."

The philosophy of discipline in this school has been made clear by the tone and content of the suggestions. We need to read statements of this type from time to time to remind us of how great the gap is between what we know is right and what we actually do in schools.

A contrasting philosophy has been expressed in a guidelines statement frequently distributed by Dr. Jo Ann Shaheen (see Chapter 8) for parents and teachers. This statement is reproduced in its entirety in Figure 4–4.

Guidelines statements differ from the usual rules and regulations statements found in student and faculty handbooks. In the first place, these statements have usually not been prepared as guidelines for students. Instead, they are usually addressed to parents and teachers. Secondly, the statements reflect a philosophy—a set of assumptions regarding discipline.

When combined with a vigorous inservice education program, published statements can be a useful tool for uniting a faculty to support a humane approach to improving morale and discipline.

4.09 Help Teachers Improve the "Openness" of Their Classrooms

It may seem strange that we are advocating more open classrooms as a way of improving discipline. The popular image of an open classroom is that of chaos—everyone doing his own thing— the opposite of well-disciplined. Such, however, need not be the case. The best so-called open classrooms are orderly, well structured, and well organized.

What do we mean by "Open Education"? Vincent Rogers and Bud Church (11, p. 34) describe it, in part, as follows:

In open education the teacher is less content-centered and more person-

Guidelines for Discipline*

"These Rules Don't Change"
Jo Ann Shaheen

1. Don't disapprove of what a child is—disapprove of what he does.
2. Give attention and praise for good behavior, not bad behavior.
3. Parents should allow and encourage discussion, but the parent makes the final decision.
4. Punishment should be swift, reasonable, related to the offense, and absolutely certain to occur—it does not have to be severe. (I'd define punishment as consequences).
5. Throw out all rules that you are unwilling to enforce, and be willing to change rules if you think it reasonable to do so.
6. Don't lecture and don't warn—youngsters can remember things they think are important to remember!
7. Don't feel you have to justify rules, although you should be willing to explain them, (and listen to their side).
8. As your youngster gets older, many rules may be flexible and subject to discussion and compromise; however, on those few rules you really feel strongly about, enforce them even if other parents have a different rule.
9. Allow the child or youth to assume responsibility for his decisions as he shows the ability to do so.
10. Don't expect children to show more self-control than you do as the parent.
11. Be honest with your youngster—hypocrisy shows.
12. The most important thing in your youngster's self-image is what he thinks you think of him, and his self-image is a major factor in how he acts and what he does.

Have you heard most of this before? If the schools and the parents could work within these guidelines for discipline, how much more of a chance our youngsters might have to become positive citizens, productive people, and happy human beings.

---

*Originally published in a booklet for the use of the Youth Service Bureau of San Diego and the San Diego County Probation Department.

Figure 4-4

centered. His or her task is to set up opportunities for learning experiences, both in and out of the classroom, where he or she can watch children and see what they respond to. While she or he has a good idea of the possibilities within the experiences she or he has set up, the actual questions brought to the materials or the activities by the children become the basis for the curriculum and much of the teacher's time is spent helping children pursue those questions, helping them to structure their learning. Consequently, curriculum is generated out of where the children are and what they bring to the situation and is not predetermined. It is difficult to test for this and even more difficult to grade it. No distinction is made between affective and cognitive development. Correct answers aren't so important as good questions; pursuing questions often results in dead ends which are not mistakes, and certainly not failures, but part of learning. This tends to minimize competition and promote collaboration.

. . . . Because the teacher cares about the children there are limits to their behavior . . . . For the open teacher what a child *is* is ultimately more important than what he *knows.*

The Rogers and Church book from which the above passage is quoted might be used as one of many basic resources for those teachers on your staff who want to become more open. You can help such teachers by putting them in contact with materials and resources, providing them with consultants, helping them plan their programs, and helping them gain parent and pupil understanding and support.

Research cited in the Rogers-Church book indicates that, contrary to much popular opinion, discipline problems are minimal in open classrooms. Furthermore, children who direct much of their own learning achieve as well as those taught in teacher-directed classes (11, p. 85).

In a summary of the research on open education, the following statement is made:

The conclusion to be drawn from this research indicates that while relatively low achievement motivation in school is related to a lack of independence and choice on the part of the child, children who have independence and self-direction will develop higher achievement motivation, fewer discipline problems, and more effective learning. Independence and self-direction are fostered in the open classroom.

We recall that a few years ago in San Francisco, during a wave of student violence in the high schools, a TV reporter interviewed a group of students at Opportunity II, an open, street academy-type school. The reporter was attracted to the school because he had heard that there was no violence and few discipline problems there and he was curious about how the school was different from the others.

This dialog from the interview expresses a lot about why open schools are free of violence:

The reporter asked, "Have any of the students in this school ever hit any of the teachers?"

The students looked at one another with puzzled expressions. The question clearly surprised them. Finally one of them responded—

"Of course not. Why would we do that? Our teachers are our friends."

Open-type alternative schools are notoriously free of discipline problems.

It may be, however, that in your school open classrooms should be offered only as an option to parents and pupils. Pupils are not helped to assume responsibility for their own actions by being placed in open environments against their parents' wishes.

4.10 Organize Task Forces for Systematic Planning and for Problem Solving

Another way you can help teachers improve discipline in the school is through organizing task forces which involve them directly in planning and problem solving. Several such task forces can be operating simultaneously in a school. The only limit is the amount of time staff members and students are willing to devote to school improvement and the amount of time the administrator can spend in coordinating and supporting their activities.

Membership on task forces is usually open to anyone willing to work for school improvement—pupils, teachers, parents, non-certificated staff, and administrators. A task force assumes responsibility for studying a problem and *then solving it* by applying a previously agreed-upon problem solving process.

One of the principal's jobs is to assist task forces in learning how to apply the problem solving process. He also functions as a member of the group, helping the group structure its activities and helping them apply their solutions by removing administrative debris from their path. He is a teacher, a facilitator, and an organizational specialist.

It is not difficult to teach groups to master the problem-solving process. Dr. Jo Ann Shaheen's teachers in an elementary school in

New York (see Chapter 8) learned the process and then taught children to use it.

The process consists of seven steps as defined in Figure 4–5.

● Step 1 *Sensing the Problem.* It is possible that the presence of a problem may be sensed before the task force is organized. Some school administrators make special efforts to sense problems while they are small enough to be managed easily. An undetected problem may grow into a crisis. Techniques for sensing problems include:

- Surveys of pupil, staff, and parent opinions
- Small and large group meetings, e.g., meetings with parents in homes, student council-sponsored problem-sensing meetings, and faculty meetings
- Use of climate analysis instruments such as the CFK Ltd. School Climate Profile (3)

There will be a tendency, during the problem sensing stage, for individuals to begin suggesting solutions. When this happens, whoever is in charge of the session should explain that solutions are best proposed after a problem is defined. Solutions offered, however, are accepted, written down, and filed in a "Solution Bank." When the problem solving group reaches Step 4 (Inviting Solutions), all ideas in the bank are resurrected and considered.

● Step 2 *Data Gathering.* This step, plus Step 3, is often called "defining the problem." During this time the task force seeks information regarding the nature of the problem. For example, in studying the causes of discipline problems in the cafeteria the task force may wish to interview the cafeteria monitors, cooks, the manager, school counselors, and some of the pupils who have created disturbances.

● Step 3 *Clarifying the Problem.* At this stage the task force asks itself what the information they have gathered means. Is, for example, lack of supervision in the cafeteria a major cause of discipline problems? Is the attitude of the monitor a cause of pupil misbehavior or a result of it? Everyone says the food is bad. Is it? Lots of people say the room is depressing. Is it?

At this point a clear definition of the problem should be written down and agreed upon by the group.

● Step 4 *Inviting Solutions.* Now the task force is ready to consider possible solutions. Beginning with the solutions which have been collected in the solution bank, the group considers all

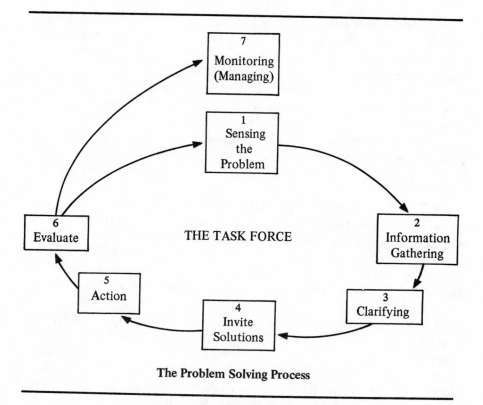

The Problem Solving Process

Figure 4–5

possibilities. They then group these possibilities into clusters and classify them under such headings as:

- Improve supervision
- Improve physical environment
- Improve quality of the food
- Revise rules and regulations
- Improve psychological climate

These recommended solutions are then written down and discussed. One key question to be considered as each solution is discussed is, "If this solution were acted upon, what would be the likely result?"

Other questions: "Do we have the human and material resources to implement this solution?" and "Which solutions are most likely to lead to the solving of our problem with the least expenditure of time and money?" and "Is this proposed solution manageable over a long period of time?"

The result of this discussion is a decision on the part of the task force that they will act on one or two of the solutions they have considered.

There is a tendency, at this point, for the task force to try to work on too much at the same time. Discourage them from doing this. It is better to do two things well than five or six things badly or not at all.

● Step 5 *Action.* At this point the task force may wish to expand its membership to include others willing to help. If, for example, the task force decides to brighten up the cafeteria by painting murals, the art teacher and some art students might join the group. If the task force decides to conduct a "clean up after yourself" campaign, they may enlist the help of a service club or the student council.

Each major action group should have a written action plan which specifies who will be responsible for what. The action plan should also define how the success of the project will be evaluated. It might be agreed, for example, that the mural-painting project will be declared a success when three murals have been completed and the art teacher expresses satisfaction regarding their quality.

It is best to restrict action to only one or two projects which are highly visible and easily achievable. Once one or two projects have been completed additional projects can be launched.

● Step 6 *Evaluation.* Informal evaluation occurs all of the time. Formal evaluation, however, should be carried out as each project completes its planned activities. The most usual type of evaluation is some type of check list which will provide an opportunity for a wide variety of people to express their views regarding the success (or lack of it) of the project. Check lists should be open-ended. That is, respondents should be invited to add items to the list. There should also be a place for comments and suggestions for future activities.

● Step 7 *Monitoring—Managing.* There is a strong tendency for problems not to stay solved. Therefore the task force needs to consider ways to manage the solutions to the problem so that erosion of the results of their efforts does not take place. If, for example, pupils have painted murals, how will they be protected from vandalism? If the initial "clean up after yourself" campaign resulted in 80% fewer trays left on tables, how can this happy situation be maintained?

The tendency at this point is for the task force to delegate the monitoring to someone else, probably the principal. The principal, of course, should agree to help. One difference, however, between a task force and a committee is that a task force *accepts responsibility for implementing its own action plans.* This includes managing the solutions once they are installed.

For example of how all of this can work, see Chapter 8.

SUMMARY

A school can be shaped up only if everyone works at it. Teachers need help in managing their classrooms, and there is much an administrator can do to help them do so. The administrator must, however, first demonstrate that he knows what he is talking about. The best way for him to do this is by being useful in the classroom.

A strong inservice program is a key to systematic school improvement. Little improvement is likely if the people involved are not able to implement what is known about human behavior. The theory-practice gap in education is immense. It can be bridged best through action-oriented inservice programs.

But many discipline problems occur in places other than classrooms. Problem solving task forces can be organized to help teachers assume leadership in solving nonclassroom problems. Teachers will work on such task forces if they are convinced that their work will result in substantial improvement in pupil behavior. After all, if Johnny has been making everyone miserable in the cafeteria for the past half hour, he will not be easy to manage in any teacher's classroom.

A good school is a place where everyone learns and everyone teaches. It is also a place where everyone helps to solve problems. By involving lots of people in making the school a better place the administrator improves morale, raises self-esteem, and reduces discipline problems.

That's what we mean by "shaping up a school."

Turning Losers into Winners– Unrigging the School

5

This chapter is based on the assumption that our schools are "rigged" in such a way that, by their very nature, they produce a certain number of losers. Everyone can't win in school because the system demands failure.

Our losers, then, who to some degree have been created by the school, tend to turn against the system. As they get older and wiser, they begin to understand what has been happening to them. It is at this point that they become discipline problems, expressing their frustration by tearing up the school, beating up on their fellow pupils, retreating into truancy, and playing games with the school authorities.

Perhaps, at least for the time being, we need to continue our remedial programs for unsuccessful, mixed-up pupils. Equally needed, however, are remedial programs for the schools themselves. We need to modify our schools in such a way that we stop creating our own discipline problems. We need to unrig our schools.

HOW OUR SCHOOLS ARE RIGGED

In this chapter we identify seven ways that our schools are rigged. You and your faculty can no doubt identify additional ways if you use this chapter as a stimulus to discussion.

Six of the more obvious components of rigging are identified as:

- *The graded school* which assigns pupils to classes on the basis of their age. In the graded school successful pupils are permitted to "pass" and unsuccessful pupils are retained or remediated.
- *Standardized testing programs* which are designed to identify winners and losers. A loser is defined as one of a certain percentage of pupils destined to do poorly on the test.
- *Strong emphasis on competition* in schools as a way of screening out the "least fit" pupils. This practice is often justified on the grounds that we must prepare pupils for our dog-eat-dog society by teaching them to handle failure in a dog-eat-dog school.
- *The use of artificial rewards*—including stars on a wall chart, tokens, letter grades, school letters, membership in honor societies, honor rolls, and pins given out in awards assemblies—all depriving pupils of the opportunity of learning for the right reasons.
- *The letter grading system* which forces teachers to communicate messages of unworthiness and failure to pupils on a regular basis.
- *Grouping and ranking practices* which continuously remind our least successful pupils that the school thinks some pupils are better than they are.

All of these practices are very satisfying to the winners and to their parents. A principal can declare war on them only if he has ambitions of becoming an ex-principal. Nonetheless, such practices have the effect of polarizing the school and creating losers and discipline problems at an early age.

In addition to these six more obvious forms of rigging, we have a seventh much more subtle component—the social system among pupils. This system typically consists of a highly structured hierarchy of cliques.

The composition of these cliques, the names given to them, and their place in the hierarchy varies from school to school. Most schools have their equivalents of "eggheads," "greasers," "cowboys," or "jocks." The clique composition of a school parallels, with some distortion, the clique structure of the community. It is there, in every school, always impenetrable, always communicating a message of unworthiness to some pupils, always creating winners and losers.

One junior high school we know has the practice of inviting its honor students to dinner once a year. Likewise, the same school invites its athletes and cheerleaders to dinner at the end of each season. How does it feel not to be invited?

How does it feel to be frozen into a clique—to belong to one clique and want to belong to a different one?

How does it feel to be frozen out of all of the cliques and to be without friends at the age of 6, 12, or 16?

How does it feel to be told, subtly, of course, that you need to be remediated?

How does it feel to be identified, to yourself and your parents, as being in the lower quartile nationally on a standardized reading test?

How does it feel to graduate 123rd out of a class of 127?

William Purkey (20) of the University of Florida has written a powerful little book on the relationship of a child's self-concept to his achievement in school. In this book he summarizes hundreds of research studies which lead him to conclude that "there is a continuous interaction between the self and academic achievement, and that each directly influences the other" (p. 23). That is, not only does poor achievement adversely affect a child's self-concept, *a child's low-self concept will also cause poor achievement.*

Samuel Proctor's downward spiral (see Chapter 1) then begins to function. The child's school environment communicates subtle messages of unworthiness. The child responds by achieving less. His lower achievement then reinforces the low self-concept, and we have created another loser.

UNRIGGING THE SCHOOL

What then, can school administrators and their staffs do to lessen the effects of those practices which harm pupil self-concept? The unrigging process must be a cautious one. Our communities are not tolerant of educators who modify long-standing social practices in schools—even if these practices create some of the problems we would all like to solve. The parents of winners are very often powerful people in the community, capable of checkmating any educator's attempt to widen the winners' circle. To them, widening the circle smacks of "lowering standards." The underlying assumption of this point of view is that standards are highest when only a few people can achieve them.

Yet much can be done, with the cooperation of staff, parents, and pupils, to moderate the harmful effects of rigging. Following are some suggestions you might try in your school.

5.01 Modify Your School's Graded Structure

B. Frank Brown (3, p. 29) has pointed out that the graded school is a Prussian, not an American idea. It was brought to this country by Horace Mann in the mid-1800's and subsequently introduced as an innovation by the Quincy School in Boston. It is, in a sense, un-American.

Because the graded organization ignores individual differences, it causes failures. It is an organizational plan devised to separate winners from losers so that Prussian and nineteenth-century American society could limit social mobility. The curriculum was conveniently rigged so that working class and immigrant children would not pass. Those who did pass went on to higher education, which prepared them to take their parents' place as members of the middle or upper class.

Following are some suggestions for modifying this inhumane system:

● Form multi-age classes and offer them as alternatives in your elementary school. Organize continuous progress curricula within the multi-age classes.

● Develop learning laboratories (see Chapter 7, p. 153) where pupils of all ages can work together on projects of special interest.

● Offer independent study programs (see Chapter 7, p. 150) which encourage pupils to initiate, plan, and evaluate their own learning.

● Encourage teachers of graded classes to offer different assignments to different pupils and to sub-group pupils within the class. Pupils can be sub-grouped according to interest, learning style, topic being studied, or diagnosed need.

● Encourage teachers to provide, at the end of group-paced, structured units, a period of a day or two for independent study activities. Encourage them to offer at least three levels of activities —some activities which are largely teacher-directed, some which are somewhat more student oriented, and some in which the student is completely responsible for his own learning.

B. Frank Brown (2, p. 60) has called these three levels, Quest I, Quest II, and Quest III. Students with a high "quest quotient" should be encouraged to contract for Quest III type experiences.

The characteristics of a quest quotient, according to Brown (p. 61) are:

Imagination

Viable Notions

Intellectual Excitement

Purpose

Power of Motivation

● In secondary schools, offer as many subjects as possible to all students, regardless of their age or class. Most secondary schools offer open enrollment for a small number of courses such as art, chorus, or the first year of a foreign language. This practice can be expanded painlessly to many more course offerings.

● Form a staff task force to study nongradedness and to initiate one or more projects in your school. Examples of successful programs include the Ridgewood High School, 7500 West Montrose, Norridge, Illinois (11), the Apollo Elementary School in Bossier Parish, Louisiana (15), the Nueva Day School in Hillsborough, California, (18) and the Wilson Campus School, a laboratory school for Mankato State College, Mankato, Minnesota (8). Nongraded schools almost uniformly report that discipline problems are rare. Apparently, when learning is individualized, failure is reduced and discipline problems diminish.

5.02 Humanize Your Testing Program

Standardized, norm-referenced tests are designed in such a way that half the children in our country must be labeled below average. Such tests contribute substantially to the progressive lowering of pupils' self-concepts as they go through school. These tests have been criticized on the following grounds:

- Such tests are useless for diagnostic purposes and do not evaluate a student's progress towards individual goals.

- They are also inappropriate for program evaluation, even though they are used frequently for this purpose.

- They frequently test pupils on material which has not been taught.

- They are culturally biased in such a way that white middle-class and upper-class pupils have an advantage.

- Cultural bias is compounded by the practice of giving "speeded" tests which penalize thoughtful, analytical individuals and individuals from cultures where speed is less valued than in middle-class America. Such tests also penalize pupils with perceptual learning difficulties who may know the material but cannot work through the test quickly enough to earn a high score.

- Tests are "rigged" against the "nature of thinking of all young children." Deborah Meier, open classroom coordinator, New York City, has stated (16, p. 3–5) that a 7-year old, still engaged in "pre-operational" thinking or at most in what Jean Piaget has described as "early concrete operational thinking" is simply not in the same world as the adults who fashion such tests. "It is for this reason," says Meier, "that such a child's ingenuity and good judgment are not only useless to the task but often even detrimental to it."

- Tests dictate curriculum. The question regarding local vs. state or federal control of the curriculum becomes moot when scholars at Princeton, New Jersey decide what is to be tested. If you decide what is to be tested you are also deciding what is to be taught.

- Tests often don't test what they say they do or what people think they do. The reading tests criticized by Deborah Meier, for example, test not only the child's ability to read but also his knowledge of the meaning of certain words and phrases and his ability to reason logically.

- Standardized tests are subject to gross misinterpretations. Test manuals may caution users against using the results for such purposes as evaluating teachers or programs. Nevertheless, the press and the public tend to use results in exactly that way.

- Standardized tests tend not to test for those competencies which are being successfully taught by large numbers of teachers. James Popham (19), considered a national expert on testing, has said that such items tend to be dropped from standardized tests because they do not differentiate well between groups of children. In other words, too many children have acquired the competence to make the item useful for the purposes of the test.

These and many other criticisms are being leveled at norm-referenced standardized tests. John Holt (10, p. 58) says that testing "hinders, distorts, and corrupts the learning process." In his book, *The Underachieving School*, Holt devotes an entire chapter to describing how this corruption takes place. William Glasser (7, p. 109) in his chapter on preventing failure, advocates divorcing objective

tests from the evaluation of students. The National Advisory Committee on Mathematical Education (NACOME) has condemned
standardized, norm-referenced tests and has recommended that
they be replaced with "objective-directed" tests (17). Likewise the
National Education Association has called for discontinuing the use
of any test which compares performance to predetermined norms
and is administered in identical form to large numbers of students
(6, p. 106).

How then, can your testing program be unrigged? Here are some
suggestions:

● Instead of norm-referenced tests, whenever possible use objective referenced or criterion-referenced tests. These tests, if used
carefully, will test only material which has been taught. They also
have the advantage of being useful as diagnostic instruments.

● If you must use standardized tests, form a study committee
to do a detailed item analysis of those tests you are considering.
Then use the tests which come closest to matching the objectives
in your curriculum.

● Give norm-referenced tests only to a sampling of students. It
is a waste of money and an imposition on a student's time to subject
every pupil to a test when, by sampling, you can obtain equally
valid information.

● Emphasize action-oriented testing procedures which integrate
evaluation with instruction. Examples:

● Materials testing pupils' measurement skills from Education
Development Center's, Project TORQUE (4).

● Teacher's "Daily Record" for each child—a form on which the
teacher makes daily notations regarding each child's activities
and achievements (9, p. 39).

● Pupil journals—records of activities and achievements kept by
each pupil. Such records sometimes become quite personal,
revealing not only the pupil's academic but also his emotional
growth (9, p. 46).

● Use Individualized Assessment Guides (see Figures 5–1 and 5–2).
Such guides list the competencies expected of students in a
group and then provide a place for the teacher or pupil to indicate that the competency has been demonstrated. Evidence of
achievement such as tests completed, papers written, or projects completed can be kept by the pupil or the teacher in the
pupil's folder in a file drawer. Such a guide can be very open,

as illustrated in Figure 5–1, or can be very highly structured, as in Figure 5–2.

● Report test results to pupils and parents in a personal, positive, constructive way. Figure 5–3 reproduces a report sent home to parents of a pupil in the Blauvelt Elementary School, Orangetown, New York. (See Chapter 10.) The principal, Dr. Jo Ann Shaheen, wrote a personal comment such as the one reproduced here to every pupil who took the test.

Sample Individualized Assessment Guide
(open)

Daily Activity Record

Name: _____   Date: _____

Subject: _____

Activity: _____

Objective (What did you wish to learn from this activity?):

Evaluation (How well did you achieve what you set out to do?)

  Pupil comment:

  Teacher comment:

  Comment from others (optional):

Note: This form is to be filled out by the pupil on completion of an assigned or independent learning activity. Once the teacher's comments and comments of others in the learning team are recorded the form is filed along with other evidence that the objective has been achieved.

Figure 5–1

Sample Individualized Assessment Guide
(Structured)

Pupil Progress Profile*

Pupil's Name: _____ Year in School ____

Directions to the Teacher: This profile is to be used as a continuous record of the pupil's progress in mathematics. Three columns are provided. When mastery of a key concept is achieved for the first time, find that concept on the chart and mark the month and year in the first column. Columns two and three have been provided in case there is a need to retest a concept at a later date.

GRADE 4	1	2	3
152 Write numbers between 1,000 – 1,000,000			
153 Repeated addition as multiplication			
154 Basic multiplication facts			
155 1-digit × 4-digit, no regrouping			
156 1-digit × 2-digit, regrouping			
157 1-digit × 3-digit, regrouping			
158 1-digit × 4-digit, regrouping			
159 Basic division facts			
160 Identify division terms			
161 Multiplication and division inverse			
162 4-digit division × 1 digit, no remainder			
163 4-digit			
164 open			
165 open			
166 Make change from $10.00			
167 Money value in word form			
168 Sub. $ and ¢			
169 Round off to 10's, 100's, 1000's			
GRADE 5			
170 Write place value to 100,000,000			
171 Read place value to 100,000,000			

*Adapted from a profile used by Aberdeen School District #5, Aberdeen, Washington. Only the grade 4 profile is shown. The original form covers Kindergarten through grade 12 on a four-page form.

Figure 5–2

Child's Name _____ Robert Jones* _____ Date __1-3-__

Below are listed your child's achievement levels on the Metropolitan Achievement Tests administered by the Blauvelt School in October, 1975.

__6__	Word Knowledge	__4__	Math Concepts
__7__	Reading	__6__	Math Problem Solving
__7__	Total Reading	__4__	Total Math
__6__	Language	__5__	Science
__4__	Spelling	__6__	Social Studies
__2__	Math Computation		

Look here to interpret the meaning of the achievement levels:

9   Only 4% of the children throughout the country taking this test will have performed as well as your child in this skill area.

8   Your child's skills are definitely above average and are considered excellent in this skill area.

7   Test results show that your child has above average skills in this skill area.

These achievement levels show that skills are average. Fifty percent
6   of the children in the country taking this test will have scores in
5   these three achievement levels. Continuous attention to skill de-
4   velopment in this area will be necessary for your child to feel competent in this skill area.

3   Your child's test scores show that your child needs help in this area of skill development.

Test results show that your child needs considerable help to im-
2   prove skill in this area. Blauvelt teachers will assist your child, with
1   your cooperation, in the hope that there will be substantial improvement.

Bob: You have earned good scores in reading; your improvement in reading comprehension is excellent. Certainly, I am having a hard time ex-

Figure 5-3

plaining the "2" in math computation. You have good intelligence, and I think it is time that you stopped pretending and rolled up your sleeves and mastered the basic math. How about it?

Take care.

Dr. S.

---

*Not his real name.

Figure 5-3 (cont'd.)

5.03 Reduce the Harmful Effects of Over-Competitiveness in Your School

Competition is much in demand by winners and parents of winners. This does not necessarily mean, however, that large numbers of pupils need to lose consistently. One person's success need not always depend on the failure of another. Here are some suggestions for using competition to build up rather than to destroy the self-concepts of potential losers:

● Reduce competition in those activities where it is not absolutely necessary. For example, music, art, and dramatics festivals need not be competitive. Competitiveness, in fact, often detracts from some of the most important objectives of such events—learning to appreciate the results of total group efforts, for example. A pupil preparing a science project because he wants to learn about a scientific principle, then, need not be distracted from his purpose by the game playing required to get a red or blue ribbon.

● Provide a variety of activities in the school which provide for cooperative efforts. These activities can be in addition to the usual competitive ones. Examples:

● Form task forces of pupils and staff to improve the school in one important way.

● Have non-competitive exhibitions of pupil work for parents' night. The goal would be that every pupil would have one high quality piece of work exhibited.

● Organize a series of talent shows in which anyone who volunteers can participate.

● Publish several school newspapers and magazines, not just the "official" one. Invite everyone to submit items for publication and publish all items submitted. Some pupils, of course, will need individual help in order for their writing to be acceptable. Helping a pupil write for publication can be an opportunity to teach him a lot about writing skills.

- Operate a "We've Got Pride" bulletin board. Anyone in the school—staff member, pupil, or parent, who does something good for himself or the school gets his picture posted together with a description of what he has accomplished. This technique was very effective at Cleveland High School, Seattle (see Chapter 1).

- Expand the intramural sports programs. Provide, within this program, for some of the less competitive physical activities such as modern dance, skating, and recreational golf, swimming, tennis, and bowling.

- Refrain from promoting unnecessary competition in the school—putting one home room against another in an attendance contest, for example. There is a tendency in many schools for administrators and teachers to turn almost all school activities into contests. This teaches pupils that all important activities are competitive. Everyone doesn't believe this. Another example: It is common practice in many schools to turn the reading of library books into a contest by keeping a chart on which individual or which team read the most. Such a contest teaches pupils to read for the wrong reasons, i.e., to win the contest rather than to enjoy good writing. It also places slow readers in a "rigged" situation—that is, a situation in which they are predestined to lose.

5.04 De-Emphasize the Use of Artificial Awards

The giving of artificial awards, like over-competition, may distract the pupil from achieving because he wants to learn something he considers important. Several questionable assumptions underlie our current torrent of award-letting, among them:

- That what we ask pupils to do is not seen by them as being important. (If pupils felt we were asking them to do something which would be of value to them we wouldn't need artificial rewards.)

- That pupils are not smart enough to realize when an environment is being rigged to get them to do things they would not ordinarily do.

- That intrinsic rewards, the feeling of satisfaction which follows the successful completion of a worthwhile task, are insufficient motivators. Therefore phony incentives must be provided.

- That education is a process which can be facilitated by practical application of stimulus-response psychology and that human beings, if they are young enough and naive enough, will not mind being manipulated.

If you would like to de-emphasize artificial rewards in your school, you might begin by discontinuing or modifying one or more of the following practices:

- Discontinue awards assemblies in which the winners walk across the stage and the losers watch.

- Replace awards banquets with one or more potluck dinners or picnics and invite everyone.

- In place of honor rolls, which list only a few pupils, publish a complete list of all students. Then list after each pupil's name one or more of his achievements or contributions to the school. (Former academic honor roll pupils, would, of course, be included and their academic excellence recognized.)

- Do the same for "honor graduates." Everyone should be an honor graduate.

- Provide school letters, not just for athletes, cheerleaders, and band members, but for all pupils who participate for a year in an organized activity to serve the school. It would be prudent, of course, to implement this suggestion very slowly, extending the privilege of wearing a letter only to a few groups at a time. In some communities a principal can be fired for even considering such an idea. This practice challenges the traditional hierarchy of activities, i.e., that athletics are the most prestigious and that everything else is inferior.

- Reorganize the national honor society into an organization which finds and honors all pupils who are doing good things for themselves and their school. The new honor society, for example, might be charged with the publication of the new honor roll and the new, all inclusive honor graduates list, as suggested above.

- Encourage civic groups, such as the Daughters of the American Revolution, the American Legion, and local service clubs to sponsor activities which involve lots of pupils rather than con- centrating on honoring only a few. An organization, for ex- ample, instead of sponsoring an essay contest which recognizes only one to three winners, might sponsor a combined student- community "American Heritage" exhibition.

One way to reward lots of students in a genuine rather than an artificial way is by issuing honors passes, hall passes which replace the usual temporary passes issued by teachers. By issuing the pass the school is expressing trust in the student. Students who betray the trust will lose their card.

This system is operating successfully at the Hocker Grove Junior High School, Shawnee Mission, Kansas, and at the Ridgewood High School, Norridge, Illinois.

Our hope is that you devise a large number of ways to say "thanks" to pupils and staff who benefit themselves and the school. The as- sumption should not be that only a few people should be honored. This implies that those not rewarded are less honorable. Rather, the assumption should be that the school belongs to everyone and that everyone, given encouragement, will want to improve himself and his school.

One way to say "thanks" to lots of people on a daily basis is to issue "Thank-U-Grams" or "Orchids." A Thank-U-Gram is a simple form which looks like a telegram. People send them to one another as a way of saying "thanks." A sample "Orchid" form is reproduced in Figure 5–4. These forms should be so widely distributed that every- one will get at least one each year.

Such genuine, often-used procedures as these can do much to make elitist, artificial rewards unnecessary.

There may be, initially, some pupils who are not making such contributions. If so, it then becomes the concern of staff and stu- dent leaders to help these pupils become productive enough so that their efforts can be recognized.

5.05 Do Something About Your School's System of Letter Grades

That letter grading of pupils is a harmful practice is widely recognized by teachers and administrators. Yet the practice per- sists. The criticisms of letter grading include:

- Letter grades do not provide adequate evaluative informa- tion either to the pupil or the parent.

WE'VE GOT PRIDE

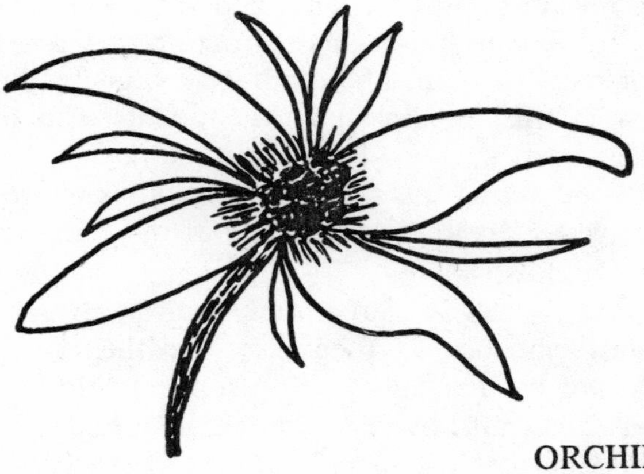

ORCHID

TO: _____

FOR: _____

_____

_____

_____

_____

_____

FROM:

THE COMMITTEE

Figure 5-4

- They are notoriously invalid. The same piece of student work may earn a D from one teacher and an A from another. Letter grading forces pupils to study the teacher to figure out what the real criteria are.

- They are unreliable. The same teacher who grades a paper "A" may grade the same paper "C" six months later.

- Letter grades, when the concept of the curve is used (consciously or unconsciously) result in a predetermined number of losers being identified. The numbers of losers and winners can be controlled by the teacher by modifying the difficulty of the test.

- Grades encourage cheating and academic game playing. Pupils learn for the wrong reasons. Grades deprive pupils of the experience of feeling good because they have succeeded at a task they feel is important.

- Grading systems discourage pupils from enrolling in difficult courses. It is widely known that many grade-conscious pupils, especially if they are college bound, avoid difficult courses because a low grade might lower their grade point average.

- Grades are unfair. Many teachers allow highly subjective factors to influence their grading. A pupil may be penalized, for example, if he wears unusual or unclean clothing, if he uses language which the teacher perceives as crude, if he comes from a minority race or religious group, or if he exhibits more than the usual degree of creative or independent thinking.

A wide variety of alternatives to traditional letter grading have been defined. Perhaps you would like to form a committee or a task force in your school to modify your grading system. If so, such a group will find Howard Kirchenbaum's book, *Wad-Ja-Get?* (13) of great value. Among the alternatives to traditional grading identified by Kirchenbaum and others are (p. 293):

- Written Evaluations. Teachers' written evaluations are sometimes supplemented with check lists and student self-evaluations. Such evaluations have the advantage of providing much more information to the learner and his parent than do the usual letter grade.

- Self-Evaluations. Self-evaluations are especially appropriate in schools dedicated to educating independent learners. Pupils who learn to plan their own learning experiences through self-evaluation also learn to evaluate those experiences.

A sample self-evaluation form, currently in use in the Viewlands Elementary School, Seattle, Washington, is reproduced in Figure 5–5. According to Mr. Herb Boies, who was principal at Viewlands when the procedure was established, the teachers wanted to encourage self-evaluation as a way of fostering an increase of student responsibility for their own self-improvement. The form is used with pupils in grades 3 through 6. Information on the form is private; it is shared with the parent only if the pupil gives his permission.

- Contract Grading. Requirements for receiving a letter grade are defined at the beginning of an assignment or the beginning of a course. Pupils earn grades by completing a predetermined amount of work in accordance with a predefined standard of quality.

- The Mastery Approach or the Performance Curriculum. Learning objectives for a course are written and for each unit of work "levels of mastery" are defined. Thus a pupil knows in advance what level of proficiency he must demonstrate to get an "A", "B", or "C". Pupils may progress through the curriculum at their own rate and make choices regarding how they will master the objectives.

- Pass/Fail Grading. The criteria for passing the course are specified. Pupils then receive a "Pass" if they meet these criteria and a "Fail" if they do not. Some schools permit pupils to take only one or two courses per year on a pass-fail basis. This practice enables college-bound pupils to take difficult courses without endangering their grade-point averages. Under this system pupils who receive a "Fail" grade for a unit of work may be given an opportunity to re-do the work until a "Pass" grade is earned. A variation of this concept is "credit-no credit" grading, in which the symbols "CR/NC" is not a failing grade.

- Parent-Teacher Conferences. A conference as a substitute for giving letter grades is a growing practice in elementary schools. This has the advantage of providing the parent with more detailed information regarding his child's progress. It also opens communications between the parent and the teacher. Some schools include the pupil in the conference session and encourage the pupil to share his self-evaluation with his parents.

VIEWLANDS ELEMENTARY SCHOOL

STUDENT SELF-EVALUATION REPORT

OF _____

We, as parents and teachers, wish for our children to be more responsible and accountable for their own growth. This report form gives your child an opportunity to evaluate, along with us, how well he is doing and where he needs to improve.

STUDY HABITS AND ATTITUDES

	YES	NO	SOMETIMES
I use my best effort when I work			
I work without bothering others			
I listen well			
I follow directions			
I try to finish what I start			
I take care of the things I use			
I work well in a group			
I work well by myself			

KNOWLEDGE, SKILLS AND APPRECIATIONS

	YES	NO	SOMETIMES
I like to share experiences			
I enjoy reading			
I read well			
I like to write reports			
I like to write stories			
I write all my work carefully			
I spell my words carefully			
I enjoy art			
I enjoy music			
I like physical education			
I am a good sport			
I enjoy math			

I would like to learn more about _____

_____

_____

Figure 5-5

Comments _____

_____

Grades 3, 4, 5, 6

_____

Figure 5-5 (cont'd.)

All pupils do not have to be evaluated in the same way. Viewlands Elementary School in Seattle, previously mentioned in this chapter, offers parents five reporting options:

1) *Goal Setting Conferences.* The teacher and parent meet at the beginning of the year to agree on specific goals to be accomplished. A second conference at mid-term is held to check the pupil's progress towards the goals. At the end of the year the teacher provides a written progress report.

2) *Written Reports.* The parent may choose to receive a report card at the end of each quarter. Parents may choose between two kinds of report cards. One reports conventional letter grades comparing their child with others in the same grade. The other identifies specific skills gained and progress made.

3) *Two Conferences Plus Two Report Cards.* Conferences are held at the end of the first and third quarters. Parents receive a report card at the end of the second and fourth quarters.

4) *Conferences.* The parent confers with the teacher at the end of each quarter.

5) *One Conference Plus Three Written Reports.* Parents confer with the teacher at the end of the first quarter and receive a report card at the end of the other three quarters.

According to Mr. Boies, during the first year of implementation most parents selected alternative #5 (one conference plus three written reports) with a slightly higher percentage of parents opting for the criterion-referenced report form as opposed to letter grades.

Teachers support continuing the policy; however, they would like to see the number of options reduced from five to three.

Mr. Boies suggests that anyone trying to organize such a program should allow a year for planning and involve teachers and parents intensively in the writing of the policy.

Figure 5–6 reproduces the form which Viewland parents use to register their choice of evaluation procedures.

One valuable resource on grading practices is the January 1975 issue of *Educational Leadership* (5). The entire issue is devoted to articles on "Alternatives to Grading." Another excellent publication is ASCD's *Degrading the Grading Myths* (21) which identifies a variety of alternatives to conventional grading practices.

5.06 Modify Your School's Grouping and Ranking Practices

One way we rig our schools to create failures is by creating low-ability or "homogeneous" groups and then assigning pupils

---

Viewlands Elementary School
Seattle, Washington

STUDENT'S NAME _____

TEACHER'S NAME _____ ROOM NO._____

I have decided that the basis for reporting during the coming school year is:

☐ A. Alternative 1. Goal Setting Conferences
☐ B. Alternative 2. Written reports each quarter
☐ Option I
☐ Option II
☐ C. Alternative 3. Two conferences plus two report cards
☐ Option I
☐ Option II
☐ D. Alternative 4. Conferences each quarter
☐ E. Alternative 5. One conference, plus three report cards
☐ Option I
☐ Option II

If in the event that this form is not returned, the *teacher will select* an option for reporting the student's progress. Please return this form to the classroom teacher by October 3, 1973.

Thank you.

H. E. Boies
Principal, Viewlands

Figure 5–6

to them on the basis of their performance in class and on standardized tests. Pupils placed in such groups are being subtly told by the school that they are less worthy than their peers.

The argument that such grouping practices result in improved achievement for low achievers is not supported by research. Dr. Joseph E. Bechard, Assistant Superintendent for Curriculum and Instruction in Waukesha, Wisconsin, has studied this research carefully. Here are a few gems from his study:

1) Ability grouping produces conflicting evidence of usefulness in promoting scholastic achievement in superior groups, and almost uniformly unfavorable evidence for promoting scholastic achievement in average or low-achieving groups.

2) The effect of ability grouping on the affective development of children is to reinforce favorable self-concepts of those assigned to high achievement groups, but also to reinforce unfavorable self-concepts in those assigned to low achievement groups.

3) Low self-concept operates against motivation for scholastic achievement in *all* individuals, but especially among those from lower socioeconomic backgrounds and minority groups.

4) The effect of grouping procedures is generally to put low achievers of all sorts together and deprive them of the stimulation of middle-class children as learning models and helpers.

5) Desegregated classes have greatest positive impact on school learning of socio-economically disadvantaged children when the proportion of middle-class children in the group is highest. Conversely, when socio-economically disadvantaged children are in the majority in a class, the effect of grouping is commonly to produce poorer achievement on their part.

6) Assignment to low achievement groups carries a stigma that is generally more debilitating than relatively poor achievement in heterogeneous groups.

Bechard's summary of the research on the effects of grouping make it clear that homogeneous grouping is a highly effective way of depriving children from low socio-economic families of the opportunity to succeed in school. Even in a desegregated school system these children are resegregated, labeled, stigmatized, and denied the stimulation of associating closely with middle-class children. They are frozen into the track.

Following are some suggestions for modifying the grouping practices in your school:

● Gradually replace ability or homogeneous grouping practices with individualized instruction. A highly effective approach to individualized instruction has been developed by the staff of the Wisconsin Research and Development Center for Cognitive Learning and is being disseminated by the Kettering Foundations Institute for Development of Educational Activities (I/D/E/A). Herbert J. Klausmier's book, *Individually Guided Instruction in the Multi-Unit Elementary School* (14) describes the system in detail.[1] Another helpful resource is William Bechtol's *Individualizing Instruction and Keeping Your Sanity* (1), a book which is full of practical suggestions for planning and managing such a program. For a brief summary of IGE's high school program, see Jon Kinghorn's NASSP Bulletin article (12). Homogeneous or ability grouping becomes obsolete when a school implements an individualized program such as IGE. Further information regarding IGE is available directly from Dr. Kinghorn at I/D/E/A, 5335 Far Hills Ave., Dayton, Ohio 45429.

● Open up the schedule of your secondary school so that pupils can take more than the standard four courses plus P.E. When secondary pupils must choose between college-bound, art and music, and vocational-type courses they are placed in a position of tracking themselves. In most secondary schools it is very difficult, if not impossible, for a college-bound pupil to take homemaking, music, art, or industrial arts.

● Schedule some classes only one or two days a week instead of daily.

● Combat some of the fragmenting effects of academic elitism by offering academic courses to noncollege bound pupils and by encouraging college-bound pupils to enroll in so-called "nonacademic" courses.

● Provide inservice training for academic teachers to help them learn how to design courses in their subject which will appeal to a higher proportion of students. Convince your academic teachers that their courses are important to everyone, not just the academically elite.

● Increase the number of half-unit courses offered.

In many schools, noncollege-bound pupils are discouraged from taking academic courses. In fact, such courses are planned in such a way that they do not meet the needs of noncollege-bound youth. The unspoken assumption is that academic learning is only appro-

---

[1] A variety of publications describing IGE and other approaches to individualizing instruction is available from I/D/E/A, P.O. Box 446, Melbourne, FL 32901. A catalog is available on request.

priate for the chosen few. This assumption has been successfully challenged by many teachers who have ventured to offer personalized academic experiences to noncollege-bound students. Mr. Paul Kameny, for example, a teacher in San Francisco, has successfully taught a course in classical Western philosophy to former high school dropouts.

Ranking policies as well as grouping policies need to be studied. The ranking of students for high school graduation is a particularly demeaning practice, justified, it is said, by the demands of college admissions officers.

In an article in the North Central Association Quarterly (22), Sister Mary Simpson, Principal of St. Teresa Academy, East St. Louis, describes the injustice of grading and ranking pupils. She then summarizes the results of her survey of 22 colleges and universities in the immediate area of her school. Only two of the 22 colleges reported that they would have to have class rank before an applicant for admission would be considered. Dr. Don Glines, when he was director of the Wilson Campus school in Mankato, Minnesota, did a similar survey with similar results.

We can no longer justify the practice of ranking pupils on the basis of college entrance requirements.

Following are two suggestions for modifying your ranking policies:

● Establish a no-ranking policy for graduating seniors. You may have to repeat Sister Mary Simpson's survey in order to accomplish this. A possible compromise would be to agree to furnish colleges and universities more detailed information regarding pupils' competencies in exchange for a relaxation of the ranking requirement. This would be a good project for a group of high schools to implement together. A number of colleges now have problems with shrinking enrollment. They are inclined to be reasonable regarding entrance requirements.

● Eliminate the medieval practice of selecting a valedictorian and salutatorian. Instead, provide in your graduation program for a large number of student speakers.

5.07 Open Communications Among Various Cliques Within the School

It is not likely that the school can substantially change the clique structure among students. Such structures have roots in the characteristics of the community itself. It is possible, however, to reduce the fear and hostility which some groups feel for other groups. Here are some ideas:

● Form a student-staff committee to do a study of the clique structure of the school. The charge to the group might be to identify and describe the major cliques in the school. Regarding each clique they might ask questions such as the following:

● What are the requirements for membership in the clique? How does a person gain acceptance? What does he have to do in order to stay in the group?

● What are the attitudes of this clique towards other cliques? Hostile? Suspicious? Friendly? Which cliques have informal alliances with which other cliques? On what basis do they cooperate? Over what kinds of issues will latent hostility flare into open violence?

● To what extent are the cliques segregated by race, economic or social class, or religion?

● Identify leaders of various cliques and arrange meetings for them to discuss how tensions among the cliques can be lessened and how the school can be improved.

● Encourage members of different cliques to work together on task forces to improve the school.

● Organize group counseling sessions and rap sessions to stimulate communication and understanding.

● Organize a variety of activities (see Chapter 6) which will attract members of several cliques.

Given a chance many pupils will welcome an opportunity to study and modify the social system of their school. With competent leadership, perhaps from counselors or from the social studies faculty, such studies and related activities can provide safety valves for increasing pressures among cliques. Such pressures, then, become less likely to erupt in unexpected violence.

One highly promising program to work positively with the clique structure of a school is in operation in several Lincoln, Nebraska schools. Called "Positive Peer Culture," the program provides for the formation of at least two different types of groups, the leadership group and the help group.

Membership in the leadership group is carefully selected so that leaders of each of the school's cliques are involved. These leaders then receive training in problem solving and in helping others. The idea is to use peer group leaders to influence the nature of the clique culture.

Students placed in the help group are having identifiable behavior or attendance problems. Each individual in the group is then helped with his problems by other members of the group and by the group leader.

Meetings are carefully structured and adult leaders for the groups are well-trained in the PPC process.

Most school administrators wait for a crisis to get clique leaders to talk to one another. Crisis can be averted if communication is continuous and if a well-planned program for helping clique leaders help others exists.

CONCLUDING COMMENTS

You might want to begin the unrigging process by forming discussion groups for the purpose of considering the contents of this chapter. You might then invite interested individuals to form task forces to work on one or two projects. These task forces should then be provided with a definite charge so that they know what they are expected to do. They should also be provided with capable faculty leadership so that they can proceed with their task efficiently.

This chapter has only provided a few suggestions for eliminating the causes of discipline problems in your school. Chapters 6 and 7, dealing with the extra-curricular activities program and the curriculum, respectively, will provide more.

Increasing Student Involvement
In the School's Activity Programs

6

One way to prevent discipline problems before they occur is to widen participation in the extra-curricular and curricular activities of the school. This chapter describes sixteen ways you can expand your extra-curricular programs to involve more students. Chapter 7 provides additional ideas for increasing student involvement in curricular activities.

Every school has its quota of nonparticipating, isolated students, the pupils who are "out of it." Some of these pupils have found interests elsewhere—in a variety of community, church, and other out-of-school activities. Some are involved in hobbies or are holding jobs or helping with family obligations. Others, however, are "out of it" completely. These are the pupils who have few interests either in or out of school. Many of these young people form gangs and out-group cliques. If they feel sufficiently negative about what is happening to them in school they may become truants, vandals, or amateur criminals.

Unfortunately, most of our activities programs are not organized to attract out-group members. Athletic programs often require a dedication and a level of self-discipline which many pupils can't muster. Organizations like the Student Council and the National Honor Society usually require that the student be elected or selected—not a likelihood for most out-groupers. A subtle tinge of elitism taints the extra-curricular programs of many schools. To the extent that programs are elitist, they tend to serve those who need them least.

Much can be done to encourage alienated young people to become involved in school activities. Such involvement, as it widens, will contribute substantially to reducing discipline problems. Following are sixteen ideas for including more out-group pupils in the extra-curricular programs. Each of these ideas has worked well in one or more of the schools we have surveyed:

6.01 Form a Task Force to Involve the Uninvolved

Such a task force might be sponsored by the student council. Membership might include representatives of some of the various on-going activities, several out-group members, and one or more sensitive teachers or counselors who can communicate well with uninvolved pupils. The group is charged with three basic tasks: (1) seek out pupils who are not presently involved in any school activity and encourage them to participate, (2) help new students find activities and friends, and (3) recommend the formation of new activity groups to meet the needs of uninvolved pupils.

6.02 Open the Student Council to Broader Participation

This can be done in a variety of ways. Here are six suggestions:

1) Hold student council-sponsored forums to identify problems and issues.

2) Sponsor task forces to solve problems or to manage the school improvement projects identified as desirable in the forum.

3) Open membership on the council to anyone in the school who wishes to attend its meetings. The role of the council would then be changed from that of a mock-legislature to that of a problem and issue definition group. Much of the work of the council would, as usual, be done by committees and task forces.

4) Delegate to the council a specific set of tasks and provide the council with a budget to accomplish the tasks. One student council we know was delegated authority to manage the student activity budget with the understanding that vandalism costs would be paid from that budget. Vandalism costs were reduced by 85% in one year.

5) Form a completely new student government each year or operate more than one governmental organization in the school at the same time.

6) Offer student council as a mini-course, as is done in Springport, Michigan (3). The Springport idea:

- Students who have not served previously on the council are given the first opportunity to run for election.
- Those elected form a class which studies parliamentary procedure, committee work, values clarification, and government.
- On one day a week the class meets as the student council. A new class is formed each nine weeks.
- Officers serve for the entire year to provide continuity to the council's activities.

Ross Stephenson, Principal, reports this way of organizing the council makes it possible for more than half the students to serve as representatives by the time they leave school.

6.03 Schedule More Activities Within the School Day

The conventional activity period has drawbacks which can be remedied through utilizing modern scheduling techniques. It is now possible to schedule individual activities or clusters of activities to meet once or twice a week. We no longer need to schedule all activities to meet at the same time if we don't want to. Scheduling activities during the school day makes such activities available to students with out-of-school obligations and interests. It also alleviates the problem of the student who wants to participate but must rely on a school bus for transportation home. It is well-known that students who must ride school buses, especially those from low-income, one-car families, are functionally excluded from many extra-curricular activities by the bus schedule.
Some suggestions:

1) Organize activity afternoons for from one to four days a month. Parents, teachers, and pupils offer a variety of activities during the afternoon and pupils sign up for those of interest. Activities might include various arts and crafts, in-depth academic activities, science exploration, model building, library club, or "learning about the world through stamp collecting." Such a program operates successfully in the Yankee Ridge and Thomas Paine Elementary Schools in Urbana, Illinois.

2) Provide an inter-disciplinary team of teachers with a block of time and a large group of pupils and encourage them to build activity schedules into the block.

3) Add a period to the school day so that more activities can be scheduled with fewer conflicts.

4) Initiate a modular schedule which provides pupils with a limited amount of unscheduled time—which can be rescheduled for participating in the activities program.

6.04 Reduce "Hidden Tuition Costs"

One reason frequently given for limited participation in a school's activity program is cost. Pupils from low-income families may be reluctant to admit that cost is a factor. In many cases, however, it is very significant.

Our suggestion is that you might want to form a study group to make a list of all the fees, dues, required purchases, admission charges, fines, which students must pay to fully participate in the life of the school. Ask the group to analyze the list, interview a large number of pupils regarding their findings, then make suggestions for reducing the cost barriers to participation in activities.

6.05 Operate a "Late Bus"

There is obviously a cost problem with operating late buses. In districts which can afford them, however, their use can result in an increase in participation in after-school extra-curricular activities.

6.06 Expand Student Service Activities

A few schools have written into their school philosophies the statement that every student should have a least one service experience before leaving the school. In both elementary and secondary schools such experiences can be recognized by reports home, letters of thanks, news articles, and project descriptions added to the student's personal record. Junior and senior high schools may also record such activities on the pupil's transcript or on an addendum to it. Some common activities include:

(1) Community volunteer programs. In such programs students have read to blind people, served as aides in community centers and hospitals, helped in political campaigns, cleaned junk out of streams,

and planted trees in parks and forests. For example, in Roy Junior High School, Roy, Utah, students have organized an "Adopt a Grandparent" program. Adopted grandparents are hospital patients who do not have families or whose families live long distances from the hospital. In Urbana, Illinois, high school students serve Thanksgiving dinner each year to elderly citizens who cannot be with their families.

Many community agencies, including service clubs and churches, can assist with planning a volunteer program. The American Red Cross has a special interest in promoting such activities.

(2) School service activities. All schools sponsor some such activities. The variety is limited only by the amount of energy and imagination available from your staff and pupils. Some examples:

● In the Colville, Washington, High School five student assistants help the custodian keep the building clean during the day. Pupils also pitch in to clean up the school grounds following football games.

● Some schools sponsor clean-up afternoons. Everyone takes a couple of hours off and pitches in to clean up the school and grounds. This activity is especially popular on warm spring days. It can be combined with an all-school outing or picnic.

● One junior high school student council sponsors an annual "treasure hunt." Pupils working to clean up the school or grounds may find numbered tokens stapled to some pieces of litter. These tokens can be exchanged for nominal prizes.

● In lots of schools we know pupils are forming task forces to clean up and paint up washrooms. One group of girls even tried their hand at a little wallpapering.

● Pupils in the Fisher Junior High School, Urbana, Illinois, with leadership from their art teacher, painted murals depicting human relations themes. Each pupil was given an opportunity to paint his own ceiling tile with a design of his own choosing.

● At the Indian Grove School in Mt. Prospect, Illinois, fourth grade pupils serve as "buddies" to kindergarten pupils, helping the younger children choose and check out books and frequently reading to them.

● Pupils in Roane County (Tennessee) Schools tutor younger children, serve as trained volunteers in the school's health clinic, work in school libraries, assist with scheduling, and assist with teaching foreign languages. High school students provide 1,600 hours of service per month (1).

6.07 Encourage the Formation of More Than One Newspaper or Magazine in the School

So-called "underground" newspapers need not be forced to remain underground. Publications, of course, should all operate under a well-defined school policy regarding obscenity, slander, and libel. Each publication should also have a faculty sponsor. Given sensible guidelines, however, there is no reason why any group in the school shouldn't be encouraged to publish and distribute materials.

6.08 Expand the Membership on the Cheerleader and Pompon Squads

This idea has the disadvantage of possible increase in cost for extra sponsor-time and uniforms. Membership on cheerleading squads can, however, be quickly and painlessly doubled by forming two instead of one squad for each sport. Squads take turns going to games. The number of students involved in each squad might also, in some cases, be expanded.

Mrs. Georgianna Short, art teacher and faculty sponsor of the pompon squad at the Larendo Middle School, Cherry Creek, Colorado, has a 33-member squad. She admits that it is a little difficult to train so many participants but she feels strongly that "as many pupils as possible should participate in school activities."

6.09 Remove Good Scholarship as a Requirement for Participation in the Activities Program

We realize that conference regulations may not permit you to remove scholarship requirements from participation in interscholastic athletic activities. This is, in our view, unfortunate, because it denies participation to some students who might benefit most from the benefits of athletic programs. Scholarship requirements, however, need not limit participation in other activities such as student government, academic clubs, or dramatics and music.

Where such restrictions exist, they should be removed.

6.10 Expand Your Intramurals Programs into an Intromural Program

According to John L. Taylor, the originator of the intromural concept (4), intromurals differ from intramurals in that they include much wider variety of activities and emphasize each participant's responsibility for his own and other participant's behavior.

The program is in operation at the University of San Francisco, where student participation increased from 15% of the male population to 70% of the entire university community in two years. The program can be adapted for secondary schools. Its major characteristics:

• Activities are designed and redesigned to meet the interests and expressed needs of the students and staff.

• Athletic type activities are expanded to include such sports as two-person volleyball, six-person (coed) volleyball, table tennis, gymnastics, two-person basketball, wrestling, arm wrestling, and singles, doubles, and mixed doubles tennis.

• Competition is run and governed by the performers. Volunteers assist in developing activities in which they have a special interest.

• Some activities operate in accordance with the "pure play ethic and the honor system." Many function without officials.

• A wide variety of purely recreational type activities is offered. Activities may include a variety of off-campus outings such as camping, hiking, canoeing, a day of horseback riding, an overnight snow trip, a hayride, or visiting museums, amusement parks, plays (at discount prices), athletic events.

The concept of the program is similar to that advocated by George B. Leonard in his book *The Ultimate Athlete* (2) a useful resource for any group seeking to improve an intramural program.

For information on some new experimental games, you may wish to write the New Games Foundation.[1]

6.11 Initiate a "No Cut"[2] Policy in Athletics

Many schools have successfully opened their athletics programs to all who are willing to participate. Such a policy necessitates the formation of several teams and may result in additional costs and scheduling programs. The policy may, however, enable the "late bloomer" athlete to develop into a highly competent competitor. No cut policies are especially important in junior high schools.

6.12 Organize Activities to Enhance Ethnic Pride and Awareness

Many schools enroll students with a variety of cultural backgrounds. In such schools students can be encouraged to initiate

---

[1]The New Games Foundation, Box 7901, San Francisco, CA 94120.
[2]No one is cut from the team for lack of ability.

activities designed to acquaint all students with the unique characteristics of diverse cultures. Through such activities pupils improve their self-image and their pride in their own culture. They also learn from one another that pupils of all races and cultural backgrounds are worthwhile, interesting people. Activities can be planned in such a way that they will tend to unify a school which is fragmented along ethnic or racial lines. One way you can encourage such unity is to encourage broad representation of many groups on student committees and task forces. For example, a library display demonstrating the contributions made by Spanish speaking inhabitants to American culture could be designed by a group of pupils representing several ethnic groups in the school. The idea is to encourage pupils to respect people of various racial and ethnic backgrounds. They do this by working together and learning to know one another. Some examples of successful activities:

1) An "International Dinner" sponsored by the Student Council which features different foods from different cultures. Music and dancing from each ethnic group in the school is featured.

2) Several ethnic dance groups perfect their routines, then give performances in other schools and for hospital patients and service clubs.

3) An international club sponsors student exchange programs, as international correspondence club, excursions to foreign countries, and student art exchanges. The message is that we can learn much of interest and value from all ethnic groups both at home and abroad.

6.13 Expand Musical and Dramatics Activities

Many musical and dramatics groups confine themselves unnecessarily to more conventional fare which appeals to only a portion of the students. In some ways these can be the most exclusive and elitist of all groups. Some specific suggestions:

1) Form additional small groups such as country western groups, rock groups, and jazz groups.

2) Initiate a "no cut" policy in music and drama similar to the one suggested for athletics earlier in this chapter. Make the statement that anyone desiring to participate may do so so long as they meet attendance requirements.

3) Double cast your plays and musicals, i.e., cast two people

instead of one for each part. This practice enables you to double the number of performers and increase the size of audiences. It also provides the cast with some insurance against the common disaster of an unexpected illness of a performer.

4) Deliberately choose plays and musicals with large casts.

5) Expand participation by writing in several large group scenes, even if the script does not call for them. You can also write in parts for already-formed musical or dance groups.

6) Sponsor one or more school-wide talent shows. Ask parents to help. One school we know sponsors a joint school-community talent show which includes both adult and student talent.

6.14 Lift Student Morale with Assemblies

Schools in which student morale is low often find holding assemblies extremely difficult. Thus, for some schools, the launching of a series of morale building assemblies may have to be postponed until other activities succeed in raising morale and school pride to a threshold level. Once this level is reached, however, an assembly task force can plan and manage a wide variety of inspiring, informative programs. Assemblies should be carefully planned to foster school pride as well as to entertain and inform. The planning committees should deliberately involve out-group pupils in the planning and, where appropriate, in the programs. Everyone in the school must feel that the assemblies are theirs.

6.15 Expand and Modify the School's
Social Programs

In some schools, school parties, dances, fun nights, picnics, swimming parties, and similar activities are less well-attended than they might be for a number of reasons. In some cases the activities suffer from elitism. They are planned by and for only a few students; hence, only a few students show up. In other cases such activities are overchaparoned or are hampered in their spontaneity with unnecessarily detailed or restrictive rules and regulations. In some cases pupils don't come because they don't have the money or because of transportation problems. Some schools are located in neighborhoods considered by parents to be unsafe at night. Your school's task force to expand social activities might wish to survey the students to learn about the reasons for nonattendance. Using information obtained from such a survey, they may be able to plan a series of highly successful activities. You may wish to try some ideas such as these:

1) Hold some social events during school hours or immediately after school. If possible, run buses late on days you offer after-school events.

2) Celebrate important ethnic holidays with social activities. In elementary schools, ask parents to help.

3) Teach pupils how to dance at an early age so they will feel more comfortable at social events where dancing is the main activity.

4) Combine social events with popular sports activities such as bowling or roller skating.

5) Make all social events free. Lack of money can keep some pupils away.

6) Invite local celebrities to make appearances at some social events. Disc-jockies, popular musicians, and sports personalities will often come if invited.

7) Hold some social activities in locations other than the school. An activity, for example, might be cosponsored by a community center, a YMCA, or a country club.

8) If your high school sponsors a junior-senior prom, do something to democratize it. A start can be made by reducing the cost to individuals by liberally subsidizing the prom from class funds. Other ideas:

   • Make formal dress, flowers, and other expensive non-essentials optional.

   • Provide low-cost, post-prom activities.

   • Hold the prom in the school to reduce cost.

6.16 Organize Programs to Promote More Friendliness Among Pupils and Between Pupils and Staff Members

It is sometimes surprising to learn how many pupils in a school have almost no friends. A variety of projects can be designed to benefit pupils who have few friends and to make the school a more personal, friendly place. Following are a few ideas:

(1) Organize a "Kid a Day Program" such as the one operating in the B. F. West High School in Chahalis, Washington. The objective of the program is to improve students' attitudes towards the school and

their friendliness towards one another and towards staff members. Students, teachers, and administrators who agree to participate in the program also agree to meet and visit each day with at least one student whom they had not previously known. Beyond this, they are to make note of that person's name and to follow-up the visit with daily greetings and additional conversations. Such a program has the advantage of being simple to operate and inexpensive. In fact, it really doesn't cost anything. One reported result was improved relationships between students and staff and a sharp decline in discipline problems.

(2) Launch a variety of "Make Friends with Your Principal" activities such as:

- Schedule the principal into the cafeteria during lunch hours and encourage pupils to eat lunch with him.

- Sponsor principal-pupil rap sessions both during and after school. Invite representatives of several student cliques to attend. One New York principal formed a rap session group to talk especially with the school's least successful pupils—those who frequently take home failing grades on their report cards. The result was a number of negotiated behavior contracts and fewer discipline problems from those students.

- Invite the principal to homerooms to discuss specific school issues.

- Invite student leaders to meet periodically with the principal to discuss school problems and issues.

It is our opinion that one of the best ways a principal, or anyone else, for that matter, can give leadership to the "Promote Friendliness" program is for him to become a more friendly person himself. It is especially important that all staff be encouraged to express love and affection for pupils through frequent smiles, positive, supporting statements, and warm, friendly physical contact.

(3) Sponsor "big brother" and "big sister" programs for new students. It should be the task of the big brother or sister to introduce new pupils to others who might accept them as friends, arrange for them to be introduced into several social cliques, and arrange for them to be invited to join several of the school's activity programs.

(4) Organize "Your Custodian Is Your Friend" and "Cafeteria Workers Are Your Friends" programs. Activities might include interviewing staff members for the school paper, forming study groups to

find out and report what these individuals do for pupils, and inviting custodians and cafeteria workers to meet with homerooms, the student council, or with school improvement task forces. Similar activities can promote friendliness between pupils and secretaries, bus drivers, or teachers. What would you think of a "Be Nice to Your Teacher Week"?

(5) Sponsor task forces to make various places within the school more friendly places. One project, for example, might be designed to make the library a more friendly place. Other places which might benefit:

- the cafeteria
- administrative office
- the student lounge
- playgrounds
- P.E. classes (very unfriendly places in some schools)

We hope that as you have read through the sixteen suggestions outlined above you will have thought of additional ideas which might work well in your school. If so, a major objective of this chapter has been achieved.

USING THE EXTRA-CURRICULAR ACTIVITIES CHECK LIST

In Appendix D we have reproduced a suggested "Extra-Curricular Activities Check List" which will enable you to involve teachers, pupils, or parents in identifying which, if any, of the sixteen suggestions in this chapter you may wish to implement.

Prior to completing the form each respondent should understand the meaning of the terms. For this reason you may wish to present the sixteen suggestions at a large group meeting of faculty, parents, or students. The suggestions might then be discussed in small groups prior to your asking that the check list be completed. Each individual should complete his own check list anonymously, indicating only whether he is a student, parent, teacher, or administrator.

Please note that the list is open-ended so that the respondent may add suggested projects of his own if he wishes to do so. Some respondents will volunteer to sign up for task forces. You might provide a sign-up sheet for this purpose.

Most groups will want you to report back the results of the survey. It is important that you do so. Discussion at the feedback session might center on those activities which seem to have attracted the greatest support from all groups responding. Marked differences among preferences expressed by parents, students, faculty, and administrators might also be identified and discussed. People will want to speculate regarding why differences of opinion exist among the various groups.

The objective of your second meeting might be to identify one or two project activities which have broad support and to get group consensus that task forces should be organized to launch projects in those areas.

At this point you and your staff, students, and parents will be ready to begin the real work of improving student morale by opening up your extra-curricular programs.

Improving Student Morale
By Modifying the Curriculum

7

Discipline problems decrease as student morale increases. Morale increases to the extent that students become interested and actively involved in learning activities which they believe are worthwhile and meaningful.

One way to reduce discipline problems is to modify the curriculum so that each pupil can experience success and will want to be involved in the work of the school. This chapter suggests twelve major ways you and your faculty can modify your school's curriculum to improve student morale.

All of these approaches have been used widely in both elementary and secondary schools. In fact, you may already be doing a number of the things we suggest.

TWELVE IDEAS THAT WORK

7.01 Improve Curriculum Articulation and Definition

This is the most common approach to curriculum improvement. Most school districts and buildings have in operation one or more curriculum design groups charged with the task of writing syllabuses which define what is to be taught. Courses of study may be defined as learner outcomes or as topics or concepts to be studied. Curriculum design groups can be helpful to teachers and students desiring significant educational reform. They can:

- Eliminate gaps and overlaps (repetitious material) in the curriculum.
- Recommend, in a resource guide, a wide variety of materials which teachers can use to help pupils master course objectives.
- Recommend methods for individualizing instruction so that all pupils can achieve the objectives.
- Design pupil evaluation systems which are appropriate to the objectives of the curriculum.
- Design tools and procedures for reporting pupil achievement to individual pupils and their parents.

Following are six suggestions for improving the effectiveness of such a group:

1) Define the group's tasks carefully, including in the charge to the group some or all of the responsibilities listed above.
2) Coordinate the activities of the district-level group with the curriculum planning activities in each building. Too often building-level course outlines or program descriptions do not reflect district-wide objectives.
3) Be sure that nonprescribed activities, such as independent study activities, are encouraged for all pupils. There must be "breathing room" within the curriculum so that pupils and teachers can define some objectives and learning activities which are unique to a pupil's needs and interests. A district-wide or building-level curriculum syllabus should function as a guide and as a resource document, not as a restriction. It is possible for a curriculum to be well-articulated and still be flexible.
4) Include parents and pupils in your curriculum group. Often they can make very valuable suggestions.
5) Provide the curriculum design group with adequate workshop time so that teachers learn how to implement the new curricula.
6) Avoid the common pitfall of creating massive, technical documents which no one will read, much less implement. Use highly generalized pupil outcome statements rather than precise behavioral objectives.

7.02 Expand the Curriculum Through Minicourses

Minicourses are short courses of study, usually of from one to six weeks' duration, which can be formed quickly in accordance with students' interest. They can be jointly planned by students and staff; they can be book- and paper-centered or activity-centered; they can encourage student creativity and increase the level of responsibility that pupils can take for their own learning. Such courses can offer alternative ways for pupils to gain credits, both in required and elective courses. As minicourse offerings are expanded, the opportunity for more pupils to become involved in learning activities of interest to them is increased. Most minicourses are in middle and secondary schools. They can, however, also be very effective in elementary schools in the intermediate grades.

Some suggestions for developing minicourses:

(1) Encourage the formation of task forces to design minicourses and include pupils and parents as members. In addition to having the responsibility for planning courses, task force members should also assist teachers with such tasks as finding and organizing materials, identifying resource people in the community, organizing field experiences for pupils, and designing evaluative activities.

(2) Offer minicourse opportunities for out-of-school as well as in-school activities. Minicourse credit, for example, can be given for outdoor education programs, community education programs, and service activities which have well-defined learning objectives.

An example:

One especially successful minicourse was offered by Mr. Paul Kameny, a teacher at San Francisco's Luther Burbank Junior High School. The class, described by Mr. Kameny as well-integrated, contained Filipinos, Chinese, Latinos, blacks, and children with a wide variety of European backgrounds. The course, entitled "Writing a Family History" was a 9-week course, offered as an elective to 9th grade pupils. The requirements were that each pupil write about his family's country of origin, how the family came to America, and how they survived in America. Each pupil also made a geneology chart and a map showing where his family had lived. Mr. Kameny telephoned each pupil's parents to explain the course to them and to ask them to help their children with the research.

The results?

- Histories were 30–40 pages long. Many contained family pictures.

- The quality of the writing was excellent.
- Each pupil learned how history had affected his family and in that way gained a healthy respect for history as a dicipline.
- Each pupil also learned, as a result of in-class reports and discussion, how history had affected the families of others who came from different parts of the world.
- All pupils gained in respect for one another's cultural heritage.
- Pupils and their parents interviewed relatives they had never before met. In several cases relatives sent letters and gifts and invited the pupils to their homes for visits. The course thus contributed to family unity.

"This course," says Mr. Kameny, "was an exciting experience both for the pupils and for me as a teacher. It was truly personalized learning."

Mr. Kameny agrees that such courses contribute to reducing discipline problems in a school. "You can't separate discipline from curriculum," he says. "If you aren't teaching them anything important they are going to start climbing the walls." Minicourses provide a variety of ways to vary content in accordance with student interests.

7.03 Expand the Curriculum with the
Quarter System

The quarter system is simply a new way of dividing the school calendar year. Under this system the school year is divided into four three-month terms instead of the usual two semesters. Pupils attend three of the four terms for a total of 180 days. Such a system enables a school to schedule a wider offering of courses within the school year than is possible under the semester system.

This system has been mandated by the legislature in Texas. What teachers and pupils think of the idea in one Texas district (Austin) is summarized in Figure 7–1.

Assistant Superintendent Donald H. Rich, of Dundee, Illinois, (8) reports that in his district course offerings quadrupled after the quarter system was implemented. The result was a "significantly changed and broadened studies program relevant to student needs" that was developed without many of the anxieties which are commonly associated with major curriculum revision.

What Teachers and Students Think about the
Quarter System in Austin*

Students Think the System:	Teachers Think the System:
Advantages: • Results in less wasted time by students • Offers a greater variety of interesting courses • Allows pupils more freedom in planning their schedules • Provides an opportunity to learn as much or more than before	Advantages: • Results in less wasted time by students • Offers students more choice and more variety of courses • Reduces conflicts between teachers & pupils • Enables pupils to spend less time in courses they cannot pass or in subjects which are not needed or desired • Has improved pupils' academic preparation for college and career preparation for the noncollege bound
Disadvantages: • Requires pupils to spend more time studying out of class • Forces teachers to compress too much material into the 12-week terms and limits time for class discussion	Disadvantages: • Does not provide enough time for developing rapport with parents and pupils • Calls for an increase in the number of course preparations • Compresses time so that some pupils have difficulty in pulling up failing grades or making up missed assignments

*This information was excerpted from a brochure published by the Office of Research and Evaluation, Austin Independent School District, 6100 Guadalupe Street, Austin, Texas 78752. We are grateful to Dr. Freda M. Holley for sharing the information with us.

Figure 7–1

Other common outcomes of the quarter system:

• school facilities are more efficiently utilized

• overcrowding, often a cause of discipline problems, is reduced

7.04 Expand the Curriculum to Include Outdoor
Education Experiences

The Graden Elementary School in Park Hill R–5 School District, Kansas City, Missouri, has operated an exemplary camping program for several years. Tom Mayfield, Graden's principal, describes the program as "a practical method of teaching and reinforcing various subject areas." A major outcome is that "discipline and work relations" show marked improvement throughout the weeks and months following a camping experience.

Descriptions of representative Graden activities are reproduced in Figure 7–2.

Another exemplary outdoor program is offered at Wapato High School, Wapato, Washington. This program, taught by Mr. Noah Winder, combines classroom study with field experiences for a complete semester. A summary of the Wapato curriculum is reproduced in Figure 7–3.

Many programs such as those just described are now in operation in all parts of the country. Following are some specific suggestions for operating such programs:

(1) Take advantage of the informality of the outdoor setting to involve pupils in group counseling activities. Outward Bound,[1] one of the most carefully defined outdoor education programs, integrates nature-challenging experiences, such as rafting through rapids, with group counseling. The result is improved self-concept and an accompanying improvement in the pupil's ability to assume responsibility for his own actions.

(2) Relate field experiences to academic learning back in the school. Academic learning activities should precede, accompany, and follow the field experience. Outdoor education is not just another recreational camping trip. Rather, it provides the pupil with an opportunity to see first hand how academic learning can be relevant.

(3) Use outdoor education as an opportunity for interdisciplinary teaching. A conservation unit, for example, can demonstrate how a given problem can be studied from a scientific, mathematical (statistical), historical, or aesthetic point of view. When a piece of

---

[1] For information regarding the Outward Bound concept, write the Colorado Outward Bound School, 945 Pennsylvania Street, Denver, Colorado 80203. Ask for their publications list.

Sample Activity Descriptions

Graden Elementary School, Reorganized School District #5

Kansas City, Missouri

FIELD STUDY PROBLEMS FOR GRADEN CAMPOUT

Nature hike:
  (a) Students will be given a list of 20-30 items to be discovered along
      the route. Team with the most items discovered wins.

        birds nest
        frog
        animal track, correctly identified
        flying sparrow, etc.

  (b) Listen:
      On the sign of the leader, students will remain perfectly still for
      three minutes, listening and writing down the sounds they hear,
      such as song birds, insects songs, tree rustles, etc. The team with
      the most complete list wins.

Community of Streams and Ponds: (team, 5 boys—team, 5 girls)
      Students will be given collecting vials to gather pond water or stream
      water to determine the most common microscopic organism that lives
      within the particular environment. (Students will return to the lodge
      to identify and observe specimens.) Microscopes, slides, cover slips will
      be provided.

Community of the Rotten Log: (team, 5 boys—team, 5 girls)
      Students will observe the community of the log to determine its
      habitat. Collecting vials, microscope, hand lens, etc., will be provided
      . . . (Items collected must be returned to log.)

Community Quadrat:
      Students will be given a particular area to discover or determine the
      diversity of live organisms that live within that area. They should be
      able to determine the predator and prey or organisms, the environ-
      mental conditions, the food source and food chain for the given area.

Figure 7-2

reality is subjected to study, artificial subject matter compartments
tend to dissolve.

  (4) Use outdoor education as a way of opening communication
lines across the usual clique barriers. Pupils can, in an outdoor set-

Wapato High School
Wapato, Washington

OUTDOOR EDUCATION

A One Semester Class at Wapato High School

18 Weeks

1. CONSERVATION, ECOLOGY AND PERSONAL AWARENESS AC-
   TIVITIES (2 weeks)
   a. Unit ends with a one day trip to the Cascades.
2. WILDERNESS SURVIVAL (7 weeks)
   a. Classroom preparation
   b. Map and compass
   c. Mountain first aid
   d. Two day survival trip
3. BACKPACKING AND WILDERNESS CAMPING (3 weeks)
   a. Good and bad equipment
   b. Where to buy
   c. Wilderness ethics
   d. Menu and trip planning
   e. Two day trip
4. FIRE ARM SAFETY (2½ weeks)
   a. 1st test is the State test from the Fire Arm Safety Training Program
      of the State of Washington Department of Game.
   b. 2nd test is made up from:
      1. The Hunters Safety Handbook
      2. Daisy-Hunter Education Handbook
      3. N.R.A.-Hunter Safety and Conservation Handbook
5. RECREATIONAL SHOOTING (3½ weeks)
   a. Training with Daisy B B Guns
   b. Pellet Rifle Shooting
   c. Rifle Shooting - 22 Caliber
   d. Trap Shooting - 12 and 20 yards
   e. Archery

Figure 7-3

ting, learn to know and respect people of different social classes, religions, backgrounds, and racial and ethnic groups.

(5) Use outdoor education as an opportunity to plan for school improvement. Very often school problems can be analyzed much

more openly and accurately if the group is away from the school in an outdoor setting.

(6) Involve parents and pupil leaders both in the planning and in the implementation of your program. They will offer a large number of usable ideas and you'll need their help to do all of the work.

7.05 Eight Ways to Develop or Expand Independent Study Programs

Independent study has already been suggested (Chapter 5, p. 107) as an approach to nongradedness. It can also be used as a device for adding flexibility to the curriculum. Some suggestions:

(1) Encourage pupils to form small, independent study learning teams. It is very lonely to be the only person involved in a project. Members of a learning team can help and encourage one another.

(2) Design the independent study program so that pupils may contract for very simple, short-term projects or for complex, longer-term ones. Some pupils, especially in elementary school, can sustain interest in such projects for only short periods of time; others can take the major responsibility for designing and following entire courses of study.

(3) Make it clear in the program's guidelines that pupils are expected to develop, with the assistance of their teachers, a clearly stated plan of work. This plan should specify:

- The purpose of the study
- A description of what the pupil expects to learn
- A list of anticipated learning activities
- A description of how the effectiveness of the study is to be evaluated
- An estimated completion date

The plan of work should be approved by at least one faculty member before the pupil begins his project. In some cases, especially with younger pupils, parents should also approve the plan.

(4) The amount of junior or senior high school credit to be earned, if any, should be agreed upon prior to the pupil's beginning the work. If dual high school and college credit are to be earned this must also be agreed upon in advance.

(5) Independent study activities might be offered either in place of or in addition to regularly assigned work.

(6) Incentives to teachers for accepting independent study stu-

dents can be offered by figuring such students as a part of the teacher's regular class load. It would be feasible, then, for a secondary school teacher to have as his assignment the teaching of four conventional classes of 25 pupils each and the acceptance of 25 independent study pupils. If he accepts 25 additional independent study pupils he only teaches three conventional classes.

(7) A record of a pupil's independent study activities should be kept as a part of his cumulative record. Such activities should also be listed on the student's high school transcript so that college admissions officers can see evidence of the pupil's capability of learning independently.

(8) Encourage pupils to take correspondence courses as a part of the independent study program. A number of universities, including the University of Nebraska, offer such courses.

One school which has developed a highly successful independent study program is the Paradise Valley High School, Phoenix, Arizona. This program, as reported in NASSP's *Spotlight* (5) offers a "self-study curriculum" to any student in school—gifted or underachiever—who is willing to draft a project description, secure a faculty sponsor, and apply to the administration to undertake the project. A "no flunk rule" is in effect whereby a pupil either receives a passing grade or no credit at all. Elanny T. Luty, associate principal, reports lots of student and staff enthusiasm for the program.

Another school with an outstanding program is Fruita Monument High School, a 690-student high school near Grand Junction, Colorado. At Fruita, pupils may use contracts to proceed through an established course of study at their own rate or to design, with their teacher, a series of learning activities which are not a part of the established curriculum. Pupils contract for an "A" or "B" grade by specifying in advance what they propose to do in order to achieve excellence. Learning activities may take place in community as well as in-school settings.

Additional suggestions for implementing independent study programs can be found in B. Frank Brown's book, *Education by Appointment: New Approaches to Independent Study* (2).

7.06 Personalize Instruction with Individualized Instruction Sheets—Five Suggestions

Teachers can make regular courses of study more flexible through the use of lesson plans designed for individual pupil use rather than, as usual, for teacher use. Such plans have been called "contracts," "unipacs," "Learning Activities Packages," or just plain "assignment sheets." Such assignment sheets can define a variety of activities which will enable pupils to master an objective, thus involving pupils in learning who have active as well as pencil-and-paper-type learning styles. They can also invite student-initiated activities and thus encourage pupils to become involved in independent study activities closely related to the course of study. When entire courses of study are organized in this way, pupils may proceed through the courses at their own rate and may be personally involved in planning some of their learning activities. They are involved in determining both the pace and the content of their curriculum. Individualized assignment sheets have been successfully used at all levels. When used at an early primary level they provide an incentive to the pupil for learning to read. Older pupils can be taught to develop their own lesson plans as a way of becoming independent learners.

A suggested format for an individualized assignment sheet is shown in Figure 7–4.

Remember that the individualized assignment sheet is a lesson plan for the learner, not for the teacher. Following are some ideas for implementing this concept in your school:

(1) Obtain some samples of Unipacs, LAPs, and individualized assignment sheets from teachers who have used them. It is easy to find a variety of samples, since most teachers already use such assignment sheets at least some of the time.

(2) Encourage teachers to keep their assignment sheets simple at first. You might begin by simply giving textbook assignments, then supplementing them with outside reading, tape listening, and other activities. Gradually broaden the number of learning activities prescribed.

(3) Try out such sheets with only a few pupils at a time. Initially, for example, only a couple of very bright responsible pupils or a couple of pupils having a great deal of difficulty with regularly assigned work might be involved.

(4) Develop a resource file on the unipac-LAP concept. Two good basic references are William Bechtol's *Individualizing Instruction and Keeping Your Sanity* (1) and Phil and Miriam Kapfer's *Learning Packages in American Education* (7).

(5) Visit several IGE (Individually Guided Education) schools[2]

---

[2] Contact your local State Department of Education or I/D/E/A for a list. For further information see footnote, page 125.

The Individualized Assignment Sheet
Suggested Format

1. Topic or Title

2. Statement of What is to be Learned
   (May or may not be worded as a behavioral objective)

3. Statement to the pupil regarding the importance of the assignment
   (rational)   (optional)

4. Pre-test (optional)

5a. Assigned activities   5b. Options for the Pupil
   - Reading Activities
   - Writing Activities
   - Viewing
   - Discussing
   - Listening
   - Experimenting

6. Description of how the assignment is to be evaluated, including a
   description of pupil options, if any.

7. Description of suggested independent study activities related to the unit.

Figure 7–4

7.07 Six Ideas for Organizing Learning Laboratories to Accommodate Individualized Instruction

Learning laboratories have already been suggested in Chapter 5,
(p. 107) as one way of helping to ungrade a school.

Learning laboratories may be defined as classrooms which have
been specially designed for active learning. We are accustomed to
such laboratories for science, art, industrial arts, physical education, and homemaking. Action learning is equally important in the
language arts, foreign languages, social studies, and mathematics.

Learning laboratory areas can be designed as a part of conventional classrooms or can be located in separate areas with a wide variety of equipment and learning materials. The idea is that learning, even highly academic learning, can take place through a combination of physical, "hands on" activities and the more traditional reading, discussing, and writing activities.

Some suggestions for establishing learning laboratories in your school:

(1) Do not organize such laboratories as dumping grounds for disruptive pupils. Learning laboratories are good places for all pupils. If they are seen mainly as remedial places or places for behavior problems, many pupils will not go there voluntarily.

(2) Organize learning laboratories as a regular part of the instructional program, not as "extras." A pupil in a secondary school may, for example, spend three periods a week in his regular classroom and two in the math lab. In elementary schools learning laboratories can be operated as a part of a team teaching program. Few schools can afford learning laboratories in addition to regular classroom instruction.

(3) Staff the learning laboratory with a team of teachers, a clerical assistant, and one or more volunteers. The learning lab staff must be well-trained in the techniques of individualizing instruction.

(4) Provide the laboratory with a wide variety of instructional materials.

(5) Provide for frequent planning meetings between laboratory teachers and nonlaboratory teachers so that their efforts are coordinated.

(6) Try eventually to organize multi-disciplinary learning laboratories. It is much more efficient to operate a humanities learning laboratory than to operate a language arts lab plus a social studies lab.

7.08 Provide for Curriculum Enrichment Activities— Five Ideas

Many schools have increased student involvement by setting aside a block of time usually two to three hours each week for expanded learning activities. The content of the programs offered is determined by two surveys. The first is of special competencies of pupils, staff members, and parents. From this survey you may learn, for example, that a pupil can help others learn how to design and construct radio-controlled model airplanes, that one parent can teach gourmet cooking, that another parent can conduct a great books seminar, and that a teacher can teach geography through stamp collecting. There is, of course, no way to predict the kinds of competencies which the first survey will reveal. They will, however, vary widely. The second survey is designed to determine how much student interest exists in each of the competencies identified. Activities are then scheduled during the student structured time so that people with expertise and interest to share are joined by pupils who have an interest in participating in the learning activities offered. The more activities offered, the smaller and more personal the groups will be.

Such curriculum enrichment programs provide for helpful and meaningful parental involvement in school activities, can provide a variety of leadership opportunities for pupils, and can encourage and support independent study projects. The idea has worked successfully in both elementary and secondary schools. Provision may be made for quality control of the activities by requiring approval of all proposed activities by a faculty-student committee.

One such program, organized at the Graden Elementary School, mentioned earlier in this chapter, offers 28 enrichment experiences including:

- baby sitting training
- horseless horsemanship
- carpentry
- junk sculpture
- modern jazz dance
- good grooming

One-hour sessions are offered on four successive Fridays in April. Over seven hundred pupils participate each year in activities offered by fifteen adult volunteers, six high school students, and forty elementary school teachers. Among the outcomes were 45 science fair projects, a newly landscaped court yard with fish pond (compliments of the gardening class), and a lot of excitement and positive feelings about learning.

A similar but broader program is offered in the same district in the Park Hill High School. Each spring Park Hill students may choose from over 90 different offerings. Activities are scheduled in the school, in the community, and in various locations outside the community. The program operates during the week prior to the spring break. A sample list of activities is reproduced in Figure 7–5.

Reorganized School District #5

Kansas City, Missouri 64152

Park Hill High School

Interim Curriculum Program

Sample Activities

100 Series—On Campus
  101 Football—Classroom and field experience plus a visit to a college football team during spring practice

  102 "Sound and Sense"—An exploration of modern music lyrics as the poetry of our time

  109 "FLICK-O-RAMA"—Production of a 16mm sound movie

  114 Grammar for College English—How to avoid college "Bonehead English" courses

200-300 Series—Off Campus

  200 Church Life—A Minister's Perspective—Three days with a local minister—2 students

  205 Air Traffic Controller—Three days in the control tower—2 students

  214 The Country Gallery—Work in an art gallery—3 students

  300 "Here Come Da Judge"—Visits to three different courts—10 students

  320 Can You Dig It—Work with an archaeologist on a dig site—20 students

Out of Community Activities

  BEACH COMBING—A trip to Corpus Christi to study marine life—cost $150, 20 students

  MEXICO CITY—A week long trip to study the history, culture, and language of Mexico—cost $360, 28 students

  NEW ORLEANS—A study of French and Spanish influence in North America—cost $115, 39 students

Note: These descriptions of activities were excerpted at random from more than 90 offerings listed in the Park Hill High School Catalog.

Figure 7-5

Some suggestions for organizing and operating curriculum enrichment programs:

(1) Involve parents, pupils, and community representatives in the planning. The Graden Elementary program, for example, is sponsored and financed by the Graden PTA.

(2) Whenever possible relate the activities to classroom studies which have preceded or which will follow the experience. Many community-based secondary programs, for example, can be a vital part of the school's career education program.

(3) Build some of the more successful activities into the regular school curriculum. Minicourses can be designed around many enrichment experiences and many other experiences can be built into units within regular courses.

(4) Expand some of the more successful career-related experiences into internship programs which provide in-depth experiences in businesses, industries, and governmental agencies. The Denver public schools operate an outstanding program of this type.

(5) Expand the enrichment program into a full-blown community-school program such as is advocated by the Mott Foundation in Flint, Michigan. Such a program provides for extensive use of community facilities by the school, use of school facilities by community agencies, and direct involvement of parents in the learning of their children.

7.09 Five Suggestions for Organizing Small Discussion Classes (Seminars)

Small discussion classes may be planned for in-depth discussion of ideas and issues or for teaching pupils to be more responsible. Such groups may be scheduled as a part of a regular course of study or scheduled apart from regular courses to accommodate special interests. Groups may meet once or twice a week on a series of related topics. Small groups are appropriate wherever discussion is an important learning activity. The size of the group should not exceed 15 students. Discussions are generally well-planned and may be highly structured. Individual student involvement in small group sessions is, however, very intense. Because of this intense involvement such groups almost never experience discipline problems. Some suggestions for organizing discussion classes:

(1) Start by offering discussion groups as a curriculum enrichment activity, then expand the program into the regular curriculum.

(2) Start by dividing regular classes into two or more discussion groups.

(3) Modify the school's schedule to provide for one or two discussion groups for each student each week. Some groups can be offered instead of regularly scheduled classes. Others may be offered as optional experiences in addition to regular classes.

(4) Schedule several groups to meet with the school counseling staff to assist pupils with resolving personal problems.

(5) Use small groups to help pupils learn to control their own behavior and assume more responsibility for their own learning. Several programs have been developed which trained teachers and counselors can use in the small group setting. Three such programs, achievement motivation training, human potential group training, and eliminating self-defeating behavior training are described in detail in the pamphlet, *Developing Students' Potentials*, a publication of ERIC (12). Another program, transactional analysis, is described by Dr. Thomas A. Harris, a psychiatrist, in his popular book, *I'm OK—You're OK* (6). A fifth program, sometimes called the "magic circle" provides a variety of techniques to foster the psychological growth of children. Dr. James Olivero describes this program in his book, *Chicken Little Was Right or The Future of Education Is Now* (10, p. 75–76).

Several of the materials described later in this chapter (Section 7.12) can be adapted to small groups. Of special interest to secondary teachers is the 9–12 curriculum *The New Model Me* (11), which contains units of instruction on such topics as Behavior, Controls, Values and Change.

These materials are also adaptable for use in minicourses.

Research shows that small group instruction, when used to help pupils become more mature and responsible, can be a successful tool for reducing discipline and attendance problems in the school.

7.10 Create One or More Alternative Learning Environments

Discipline problems are rare in our country's more open alternative schools. Pupils in such schools learn to care about one another, to plan and evaluate their own work, and to assume responsibility for their own actions.

Mountain Open High School in Jefferson County, Colorado is a good example of an alternative school that works. Students at this school work at a wide variety of learning tasks both within the school and in the community. One student, for example, is doing a "cultural study of Chicanos" by spending two days a week in Denver's west-side Chicano neighborhoods. Another spends two days a week in a hospital laboratory where he is using a spectrophotometer to take protein counts of cells. Each student must complete two community learning experiences and one community service project before graduation. In addition, each student must demonstrate the ability to write coherent, well-organized paragraphs with proper sentence structure, punctuation and spelling and to demonstrate such survival skills as balancing a checkbook and filling out an income tax form.

"The object here is to teach you discipline," one student said. "But the catch is you've got to do it. No one forces you."

Principal Arnold Langberg puts it this way: "The process here is completely different. It's on the shoulders of the kids. We're basically here to serve them, not to tell them what to do."

The number of alternative schools such as this one is growing rapidly. In fact, the alternatives movement is often described as one of the most vital reform movements in education today.

Alternative programs come in a wide variety of shapes and sizes. However, most of the programs available may be classified as follows:

(1) Religious private schools offering religious training not available in public schools.

(2) Programs within schools designed to accommodate pupils from families who hold beliefs and values different from those which underlie the majority of the schools programs. For example, a school "within a school" may be created as an "open" or "free" environment in which pupils assume the basic responsibility for their own education. Or a highly directive, fundamental school type environment might be created for pupils who come from families valuing adult-imposed learning.

(3) Mini-schools may be created within the public school system to provide more open or more fundamental-type environments. Such schools offer the same type of family-choices as do the schools within the school programs described above. In Jefferson County, Colorado, for example, parents may enroll their children in the regular program, in a "fundamental" school where basic skills are stressed, or in an "open living" school which stresses creativity and responsibility. Urbana, Illinois offers the option of a multi-cultural

school which emphasizes the values of many cultures and languages. Most large cities offer a variety of street academies. Some of these are open environments; others stress vocational preparation.

(4) Alternative mini-schools may also be created for delinquent or near-delinquent youth. These schools are alternatives, not for parents, but for school and juvenile corrections authorities. Pupils generally are assigned to such schools as an alternative to incarceration or expulsion. These schools have the advantage of being less expensive to the state than youth camps or prisons and they are often more effective in improving attitudes and behavior. Los Angeles operates twelve such schools at a per pupil cost of approximately $3,000 (compared to $4,000 for a youth camp, $10,000 for a maximum security detention home, or $15,000 for juvenile hall).

There has been some confusion between the minischools described in (3) and those described in (4) above. The effectiveness of Type 3 schools can be destroyed or severely damaged if they are used by school officials as dumping grounds for delinquents. Both types of schools are effective. They are, however, not the same.

Alternative schools and programs can be highly effective in reducing discipline problems. Most such schools report reduced violence, increased pupil achievement, high morale, and low absentee rates. Visitors to alternative programs and schools are frequently impressed with the friendliness of the students, the absence of vandalism, and the pride of the students and staff in their school. It is probable that the small size of the schools, the friendly, caring personal atmosphere, and the commonly-accepted beliefs and mores contribute to high morale and productivity. Regardless of the reason, however, alternative programs and schools *have few discipline problems.*

Perhaps your task force would like to encourage the expansion of the alternatives presently available in your school or district. If so, here are a few suggestions:

(1) At the elementary level, identify two or three distinct environments within the school and describe these environments to pupils and parents. Do not label the environments. Some schools have labeled their alternatives "traditional," "fundamental," "continuous progress," or "open" and in the process have unnecessarily alienated some parents. An example of how one school, the Leal School in Urbana, Illinois, described its alternatives, is given in Appendix E.

(2) Clearly distinguish between alternatives created for delinquents and near-delinquents and your other alternatives. The alternative program as a whole should not have the image of a dumping ground. Rather, design alternative programs to accommodate pupils whose learning styles or belief and value systems are such that they can learn more effectively in the alternative setting.

(3) Encourage frequent movement of pupils between the regular school setting and the alternative setting. Pupils attending a store front high school, for example, should have opportunities to participate in some courses and activities in the regular school. It is difficult for small alternative schools to offer such courses as foreign language, instrumental music, or laboratory science. Likewise, pupils enrolled in the regular program should have the opportunity to participate in some of the more open, creative, student-initiated learning often offered in store front schools.

This frequent movement of pupils from one alternative to another is also important in elementary schools where several alternative environments may be housed in one building.

(4) Evaluate your alternative programs carefully. You will be expected to demonstrate that pupils in all alternatives are still mastering basic skills and that no single program is substantially more expensive than the others.

(5) Study carefully the literature on alternative education, especially Mario Fantini's *Public Schools of Choice* (3) and Weinstein and Fantini's, *Toward Humanistic Education* (14). Join the International Consortium for Options in Public Education—ICOPE,[3] study their publications and attend their conferences. ICOPE's list of alternative schools and programs is very helpful to planning groups desiring to visit other districts.

Most open-type alternative schools and programs report a substantial improvement in pupil attendance and a drastic reduction in discipline problems of all kinds. Many programs, in fact, report that they have virtually eliminated discipline problems. the FOCUS program at Madison High School, Portland, Oregon, for example, reports that 70% of its pupils who had previously been "poor attenders" achieved the programs's attendance objective. In addition, positive changes in behavior and significant increases in academic achievement were reported (9). Both Education II, in Urbana, Illinois, and Opportunity II, in San Francisco, report that discipline problems have almost disappeared. Such success stories are typical.

---

[3] ICOPE, School of Education, Indiana University, Bloomington, IN 47401.

The evaluation of the FOCUS program of the Harrison High School in Colorado Springs showed that after one year pupils improved in their valuing of "moral, ethical, and spiritual considerations of society." They also felt more positively than before about their peers and their teachers (but not their parents). The number of physical fights engaged in by pupils decreased by almost 50%.

Harrison Principal, Dr. Richard Krause, reports that the program has reduced racial tension and student alienation in the school. He warns us, however, that "such a program cannot and should not be expected to handle the hard-core problem student."

Project FOCUS was originally developed by Independent School District #623, Roseville, Minnesota. It has been widely disseminated.

Most large cities operate a variety of alternative programs. Philadelphia, for example, reports that 10,000 students are enrolled in 100 different programs.

7.11 Institute a "Learning by Teaching" Program— Seven Suggestions

In a school devoted to "learning by teaching" it is assumed that everyone should learn and everyone should teach. Such programs emphasize helping one another rather than competition, and pupils develop positive self-images by being of service to one another. Some schools report success in helping pupils tutor others, even in skills in which the tutor is deficient. The opportunity to help others provides a motivation to the pupil to improve his own skills. This concept has been successful with all age groups. Care must be taken in structuring the program so that it does not foster elitism. The presumption should be that all students can be helpful to others. Student morale improves as more and more pupils find satisfaction in helping others.

Some suggestions for organizing "Learning by Teaching" programs:

(1) Order a copy of Alan Gartner's *Children Teach Children: Learning by Teaching* (4). This book can serve as a basic reference for your task force or planning group.

(2) Do not limit participation in the program to your brightest, most successful pupils. There is substantial evidence that the opportunity to help others produces motivation. Highly disruptive students have been successfully used as tutors.

(3) Consider grade level as well as cross-age tutoring programs. Grade level programs, in which pupils of approximately the same

age teach and learn from one another are easily managed and the tutors are more readily available. Cross-age tutoring provides older children with opportunities to build their self-concepts by helping pupils who are less capable and less mature than themselves.

(4) Provide training programs for all teachers and pupils who will be involved.

(5) Delegate responsibility for managing the program to one person and provide this person with time for planning and management.

(6) Involve pupils in preparation of learning materials. When tutors are given responsibility for developing or selecting materials to help others they dig deeply into the subject matter and learn more about the subject themselves.

(7) Evaluate your program carefully. *Children Teach Children* offers a variety of suggestions for effective evaluation.

It is common for learning by teaching programs to report improvement in attendance and discipline as outcomes of the program. Such improvements occur both for the pupil doing the tutoring and the pupil being helped.

7.12 Improve Student Behavior Through Values Education—Five Approaches[4]

In this section we suggest five approaches for improving student behavior through values education. These suggestions are rooted in the twin assumptions: (1) that behavior, including misbehavior, results to a large extent from a person's system of values and from his beliefs regarding right and wrong and (2) that people can be taught to modify their belief and value systems and thereby to modify their behavior.

We believe strongly that superficial control techniques, such as thinking up new rules and hiring monitors to enforce them, are not sufficient. If we are to make a significant impact on how people behave in a school we need to look critically at the content of the curriculum itself. We believe, for example, that honesty, truthfulness, and consideration for others can be taught.

Values and valuing may be defined differently in each of these five approaches. In general, however, the term "values" means principles or standards of worth. "Valuing" may be defined as that

---

[4]This section and the related material in Appendix F has been written by Dr. Larry Palmatier and Dr. Jon Davis, Professors of Education at the University of Utah, Salt Lake City.

process through which we judge people, things, and ideas as good or bad.

We believe strongly that *the secret to learning is in the students' attitudes towards themselves and their feelings of power over their own destiny.* Values education can help students develop such attitudes and feelings.

We suggest that you and some other faculty leaders might conduct a survey of the many programs for teaching beliefs and values. For your convenience, we have summarized some of these programs for you.

We have identified five of the most prominent approaches, as follows:

(1) *Inculcating Values*—The teacher selects certain values to be instilled in learners, then proceeds to instill them.

(2) *Teaching Values Through Stimulating Moral Development*—The teacher encourages moral growth of students by teaching them to use increasingly complex reasoning processes.

(3) *Teaching Values by Teaching a Process of Analysis*—The student learns to make value decisions on the basis of a logical analysis of relevant information.

(4) *Teaching the Values Clarification Process*—The teacher helps learners control their own behavior by helping them understand their own feelings and helping them use rational thinking processes.

(5) *Using Action Learning to Teach Values*—Pupils base their participation in community activities on value positions which they take regarding issues or problems.

A number of programs of merit are available within each of these five approaches. Twenty-three such programs are summarized in Appendix F.

If you wish further information regarding these and other, similar programs, you may wish to order Douglas P. Superka's *Values Education Sourcebook* (Boulder, CO: Social Science Consortium, ERIC/ChESS, 1976) (13), from which the information for this section was obtained.

There are hundreds of programs in values education. The bottom line is that no single approach or program is definitive.

We believe that a school can reduce discipline problems by helping pupils learn how to understand and control their own behavior. If you agree with us, we suggest that you begin to develop your own values education program. Such a program, we believe, should engage students in the affective and moral as well as the intellectual areas. As pupils are helped to understand their own feelings and emotions and to make value decisions on the basis of carefully considered information, their behavior will improve.

USING THE CURRICULUM FLEXIBILITY CHECK LIST

In Appendix G we have reproduced a suggested "Curriculum Flexibility Check List" which will enable you to involve teachers, pupils, or parents in identifying which, if any, of the ten suggestions in this chapter you may wish to implement.

Prior to completing the form each respondent should understand the meaning of the terms. For this reason you may wish to present the ten suggestions at a large group meeting of faculty, parents, or students. The suggestions might then be discussed in small groups prior to your asking that the check list be completed. Each individual should complete his own check list anonymously, indicating only whether he is a student, parent, or teacher.

Please note that the check list is open-ended so that you may add suggestions to the check list if you wish to do so.

Most groups will want you to report back to them the results of the survey. It is important that you do so.

In interpreting the responses, look for discrepancies between responses to the *a* part of the question and responses to the *b* part. You may find, for example, that a large number of teachers feel that your school does not offer a variety of minicourses (2a). You may also find that very few teachers feel that such programs should be increased (2b). You might conclude from this information that your faculty would not be receptive to projects to implement this particular concept.

On the other hand, you may find that a large proportion of your respondents feel that your school offers very few independent study opportunities (5a), and that an equally large number of individuals would favor increasing the number of these opportunities (5b). You might conclude that projects to expand independent study would receive general support.

Of interest to all groups will be the discrepancies between priorities felt by parents, pupils, and teachers.

You may wish to ask for the assistance of a faculty-parent-student committee in interpreting the results of the survey.

At the feedback sessions you may be able to identify specific suggestions which large numbers of individuals agree should be acted upon. At this point a planning group or task force can be formed and work can begin on a school improvement project.

Achieving More Effective Discipline
By Improving Self Esteem—
A Snapshot of What's Happening
In Cottage Lane, New York

8

The most extraordinary thing about the Blauvelt Elementary School in Cottage Lane, New York is its principal, Dr. Jo Ann Shaheen. Dr. Shaheen is special in many respects. First of all she knows what she believes in. Her extensive training in psychology and her past experience as a teacher, counselor, and director of a teacher inservice center have given her a deep understanding of the learning process and motivation. As a disciple of Abraham Maslow, she believes that children come to school with basic needs which must be met before learning can take place. Among these needs are:

- the need for physical and psychological safety
- the need for love and a sense of belonging
- the need for a home and school which reflect a basic sense of order, fairness, and sanctioned excitement

These needs are considered basic because if any one of them is denied, the child's ability to learn and to grow in positive ways is impaired.

Dr. Shaheen believes that teachers must love all their children—even the least obviously lovable ones—if learning is to take place. She demonstrates her love for children by listening to them, by communicating with them openly, by encouraging professionally responsible behavior from her staff, by refusing to accept anything but a student's best efforts, and by insisting that the school's rules be followed. She believes that the expectations of a significant adult are important determinants of pupil achievement. She talks a lot about helping children earn their accomplishments. We can best help children, she feels, if we encourage them to "stand on their tip toes," while letting them know that "we are there to catch them if they fall."

Figure 8–1 lists several of Dr. Shaheen's favorite sayings. From these you can get an idea of some of her beliefs about children and schooling.

After only two years of Dr. Shaheen's leadership, Blauvelt has few discipline problems. Yet the school is not oppressive. Neither Dr. Shaheen nor her teachers "stand with their foot on somebody." Nor is Blauvelt a permissive place. There is order without oppression. What holds the place together is a lot of love and professional competence. Blauvelt staff members demonstrate their competence by applying rather than ignoring the laws of learning and by building a school climate which nurtures and nourishes people.

Perhaps the best way to describe Blauvelt is to describe a couple of incidents which illustrate how people in the school feel about one another. Dr. Shaheen describes the school's recent Winter Festival[1] in this way:

> We began our Winter Festival at nine o'clock in the gym together—all 330 of us—and I asked the children if they would say the Pledge of Allegiance and they stood up, bright and shiny to say the pledge. And when they had finished I turned around and they spontaneously broke into the singing of *America*. I was so surprised—and really it sounded so marvelous—that when they finished I said to them—from the heart—because they had gotten to me—"I just have to tell you—I think you are wonderful."

> The room was quiet except for one little boy, one of my second graders who piped out, quite loudly,

> "We know that!"

> And that started a beautiful day—three hundred thirty children and twenty adults—all outside playing in the snow for about two hours. We had a terrific time—no fighting, no accidents, no crying, no snowballs, no whining—just youngsters and oldsters having a wonderful time.

---

[1] Verbatim transcript from a tape recording.

Seven Quotes from Dr. Jo Ann Shaheen

- I think our aggressive children want us to know that they are bleeding—want us to know that they need help in meeting their human needs. We should be grateful for our aggressive children. At least they are still in there fighting for survival.

- When you meet kids' needs for justice, respect, order, and excitement, discipline problems disappear and learning takes place.

- A child with self-esteem is not a discipline problem. A child who has his basic needs met is not a discipline problem. A child with self-esteem is not cruel, not mean, not small. He does not get his or her kicks out of doing others in. A child with self-esteem is a learner. We build self-esteem as we discipline in good ways.

- Discipline problems grow out of classrooms where the laws of learning are ignored.

- If we know the child, the child becomes special to us. Sometimes we avoid knowing the child for our own survival.

- We build discipline problems by shoving children into special programs. By using a "medical model" in schools we rely too much on specialists. As a result pupils don't have time to build an authentic, meaningful, significant relationship with an adult. We are fragmentizing our kids.

- We find that as we get kids involved in decision-making more and more, the discipline problems just fall away.

Figure 8-1

The sledding, I think, will be remembered by these children forever because many of them had never been sledding before. We went sledding on cardboards and plastic bags cut into sheets and they just had a wonderful time.

While the children were drinking hot chocolate with marshmallows—provided and served by our PTA mothers—and I was standing around, one of our third grade boys came up to me. He's a marvelous kid—bright, thoughtful, sometimes quiet. He already has dreams and commitments, and he said, "You know, we do lots of nice things in this school. You're good to us."

And I said, "We love you."

And he looked at me squarely in the eye and he said, "We know that."

And that's the beginning.

Just a few weeks prior to the Winter Festival Dr. Shaheen had been presented with an opportunity to demonstrate "disciplining in good ways."

It started to snow.

So she got on the public address sytem and said something like this:

"Boys and girls, it's a lovely snow; it's a beautiful snow; and I know it's fun to throw snowballs, but you *can't throw them*. And if you do, you will lose your lunch-recess time."

Unfortunately, the children did not believe her. They had been outside only a few minutes when nearly a hundred kids were throwing snowballs.

Some of them were brought into the office, where the following dialog took place:

Dr. Shaheen: "You know, I'm really curious. Did you hear me on the loud speaker?"

Kids: "Yeah."

Dr. Shaheen: "What did I say on the loud speaker?"

Kids: "You said not to throw snowballs."

Dr. Shaheen: "Then why did you throw them?"

One Kid: "We didn't think you meant it."

Dr. Shaheen: "But I *did* mean it."

Kid: "Yeah, but people are always saying things like that but they never mean them."

Dr. Shaheen: "Well, I do mean it."

The outcome of the dialog was two-fold:

1) For the next two days Dr. Shaheen sat for two hours through four lunch periods with all the kids who had been throwing snowballs. And they lost their privilege. ("And," Dr. Shaheen says, "I lost mine.")

2) At the Winter Festival two weeks later, everyone had fun, no one was hurt, and there was no problem with snowballing.

Of the incident, Dr. Shaheen says, "The limits I had set had to be laid, in my opinion, in the setting in which we were. And the kids respected it, and we were able to go with it."

She had demonstrated to the children that she loved them enough to be firm with them when their safety was involved. The children understood this and responded accordingly.

Perhaps Blauvelt can best be described as a school which is in the process of being unrigged. It is changing because children, parents, and teachers are changing. They have caught a vision. Because one person, the principal, cares a lot about children, parents, and teachers, we now have a school in which many people care a lot—about themselves and about others. Much of Dr. Shaheen's leadership consists simply of her being herself. She knows what she believes. She has a philosophy of education which she communicates to others through the consistency of what she does and what she says. But there is a lot more to what is happening at Blauvelt than just the strength and integrity of the principal.

Many school administrators who love children and who demonstrate a consistent, humanistic philosophy fail at bringing about positive change in their schools. Dr. Shaheen is succeeding because she also has an action program. She necessarily has enlisted the aid of just about everyone in helping her with the unrigging process.

BLAUVELT'S ACTION PLAN

What is happening? At least six specific projects designed to improve the school are under way.

- A school-wide project, called EsteemPACT, has been designed to unify the efforts of parents, administrators, children and teachers towards raising the level of the childrens' self-esteem.

- The student council is being vitalized by being involved in problem solving and shared decision making.

- Children are being encouraged by their teachers and by their principal to express their feelings about themselves and about their school through writing and speaking.

- A systematic humane procedure for handling referrals to the office has been designed.

- Children are being taught, through discussion of real incidents, about how to identify and react to various kinds of authority.

- Activities have been designed specifically to create excitement for children in the school setting.

8.01 Blauvelt's EsteemPACT Project

The avowed purpose of the EsteemPACT Project is "to form an alliance with parents around the goal of helping each youngster grow in self-esteem." The project was created by Mrs. Harriet Gardner, a Blauvelt teacher. It was approved by Dr. Shaheen, agreed to by the incumbent and newly elected PTA presidents, and submitted through the District Superintendent's office to the New York Department of Education for funding as a minigrant. The grant was used to pay for the services of a consultant who conducted a series of inservice sessions for parents and staff members. These sessions were designed to help staff and parents increase their awareness and understanding of self-esteem and of ways in which they could help to build opportunities for youngsters to grow in self-esteem.

Over a one-year period, seven meetings have been held. Separate meetings are scheduled for staff (3:30–4:45 p.m.) and parents (8:00–10:00 p.m.). The consultant, Dr. Stuart Rubner, from Fairfield University, met with a committee of parents, Harriet Gardner, and Dr. Shaheen to design the meetings. The meetings included the following:

- Role playing, simulations, and communications exercises designed to acquaint participants with self-esteem and related concepts.
- Distribution of reading materials such as:
  - Briggs, *Self Esteem* (1)
  - Canfield and Wells, *One Hundred Ways to Enhance Self-Concept in the Classroom* (2)
  - Coppersmith's data on self-esteem (3)
  - Dinkmeyer's *Child Development: The Emerging Self* (4)
  - Gordon's *Parent Effectiveness Training* (6)
  - Harris' *I'm OK–You're OK*[2]
  - A summary of William Purkey's *Self-Concept and School Achievement*[3]
- Homework assignments consisting of Esteem Contracts (see Figure 8–2) and various survey instruments. An example of one of the survey instruments assigned to parents is reproduced as Figure 8–3).
- A commitment on the part of both the parent and the principal to complete a "Blauvelt School Scholastic Attitude Mini-Inventory."
- Each parent who participated in EsteemPACT, and who chose to participate in this program option of EsteemPACT, received

---

[2] See bibliography for Chapter 7, Reference 6.
[3] See bibliography for Chapter 5, Reference 20.

Blauvelt Elementary School

ESTEEMPACT - Document #2

October 2, 19 ___

ESTEEM CONTRACT #1

Between now and our October 23 meeting I will

    a. take 5 minutes each school day and discuss with my child (children) the day's school activities

    b. compliment my son(s)/daughter(s) each day on something they have done well

    c. _____

       _____

       _____

       _____

_____   _____

       Date   Signature

Figure 8–2

a copy of the mini-inventory completed by Jo Ann during her interview with the child. Parents were also supplied with a blank mini-inventory form so that they could indicate, using different colored pencils for differentiating remarks, (a) how they believed their child would mark the inventory and (b) their *own* view of their child as parents.

Parents were then encouraged to discuss their child's responses on the form with the EsteemPACT consultant, the school psychologist, or with Dr. Shaheen.

A copy of the Mini-Inventory Form is reproduced as Figure 8–4.

Seventy-five percent of the parents are participating in one or more activities of the EsteemPACT program.

Blauvelt Elementary School

ESTEEMPACT - Document #3

1. When my child brings things home from school I

2. When my child says he/she wants to tell me something I

3. When my child misbehaves I

4. When my child completes a project he/she began around the house I

5. When I am deeply involved in a task I tell my child

6. When my child wants to attempt a difficult task I

7. When my child is not understanding something I am saying I

8. When I am angry in my child's presence I

Figure 8-3

At the end of the first year of the project all Blauvelt parents were asked to respond to a comprehensive questionnaire. One of the questions was, "My child's attitude towards school this year as compared to last year is . . . ."

Of the kindergarten, first and second grade parents responding, 77% said that their child's attitude had improved. Of the third, fourth, and fifth grade parents responding, 95% said that their child's attitude had improved. Dr. Shaheen feels that the EsteemPACT program contributed substantially to this improvement.

8.02 Vitalizing the Student Council Through Problem Solving

The student council at Blauvelt, called SAC (Student Advisory Council), operates in two sections—Big SAC, composed of pupils in grades 3, 4, and 5, and little SAC, composed of pupils in grades K,

---

NAME ————————————————————   DATE: ———

BLAUVELT SCHOOL SCHOLASTIC ATTITUDE MINI-INVENTORY

1. Does ———— like to come to school?

2. Is ———— happy in school?

3. Does ———— find school work hard?

4. Is ———— a good student?

5. Does ———— usually know the answers to questions the teacher asks?

6. Is ———— a good thinker in school?

7. Does ———— have to work hard in school to please the teachers?

8. Do the teachers usually like ———— ?

9. Do the other children in the class usually like ———— ?

10. Do things happen in school which frighten ———— ?

11. Is the school work usually interesting to ———— ?

12. Does ———— like to work with the teachers in school?

13. Is ———— healthy in school?

14. Do the children in ————'s class usually ask ———— to play or work with them?

15. Is ———— big or little compared to ————'s friends?

16. Does ———— like to answer questions the teachers ask?

Figure 8–4

1, and 2. Both big SAC and little SAC members have been taught how to use problem solving techniques to solve real problems in the school.

One major problem which SAC has worked with extensively is that of student conduct on the school buses. The problem solving process used by SAC may be summarized as follows:

(1) Through discussion both big SAC and little SAC identified "bus trips to and from school" as *the* problem which staff and students should try to solve.

(2) SAC members defined the problem by making a list of what they did not like about the way people behave on buses. The list is reproduced as Figure 8–5.

(3) The problem which SAC had defined was translated, by Dr. Shaheen, into a goal statement. That statement read: "90% of the children who ride the bus will feel that it is a pleasant, safe trip."

(4) Each teacher was asked by memorandum to conduct struc-

Blauvelt Elementary School

SAC's Definition of the Bus Problem

What We Don't Like about the Way
People Behave on the Buses

1. People saving seats.
2. People pushing people out of the seats because they didn't want that person sitting down with them.
3. People teasing other people.
4. People taking people's hats or other things and throwing them around and never getting them back, and "it is upsetting."
5. People fighting.
6. People not respecting the bus drivers.
7. Some bus drivers not respecting the children.
8. Some bus drivers playing favorites.
9. People standing on seats.
10. People hanging out windows.
11. People standing up when bus is moving.

Figure 8-5

tured discussions of the problem in the class. The discussion was designed to accomplish five objectives:

- To verify whether or not all children agreed that this was the problem the school should be working on to help pupils understand the goal statement (e.g., What does 90% mean? What does "pleasant" mean? What does "safe" mean?). Teachers used brainstorming techniques with the children to help them understand the meaning of "pleasant" and "safe."
- To choose the class's "favorite" definition of each word.
- To send a representative to the next meeting of SAC with the class's favorite definition of each word
- To gain acceptance of the goal by each class. To accomplish this a vote was taken.

(5) At the SAC meeting the definitions proposed by each class

were combined into an over-all definition of "pleasant" and "safe" and the goal was officially accepted by SAC.

(6) Each class was then asked to make two lists answering two questions:

- Why might we find it easy to reach the goal?
- Why might we find it hard to reach the goal?

Teachers taught pupils to use the force field analysis techniques and brainstorming to produce the lists. The most important forces were then identified and each class sent its representative to SAC with its products—two force field analysis lists.

(7) Each class was then asked to brainstorm possible solutions to the problem. From the lists generated, each class then selected from one to three "favorite" solutions to be recommended to SAC via their representative.

(8) SAC then voted on the *one* program idea to be implemented first. SAC voted to form an *ad hoc* committee to formulate rules of conduct for riders and "guidelines" for bus drivers. Dr. Shaheen agreed to help SAC with the implementation of two program ideas even though the assignment had been to identify only one.

(9) The rules committee agreed on seven rules and four "consequences." The children felt strongly that riders who did not follow the rules should be punished. The rules and consequences are reproduced in Figure 8–6.

(10) Each teacher then led a discussion of the rules in his classroom and the children voted by a show of hands to accept or reject them. Once the rules were accepted in each class, SAC approved them.

(11) SAC members then accompanied Dr. Shaheen to the central office where they met with Superintendent Vincent Gillen and other district administrators. The purpose of their visit was to inform the superintendent of the results of their action and to ask for his help in encouraging the bus drivers and monitors to follow SAC's suggestions for making bus rides safer and more pleasant. SAC's suggestions to bus drivers are reproduced in Figure 8–7.

(12) Not to be outdone, Little SAC, with the help of their teachers, then drafted a letter to the bus monitors. That letter is reproduced in Figure 8–8.

(13) The final step in the process consisted of two parts:

- All bus riders met with Dr. Shaheen to discuss the rules and

Blauvelt Elementary School

Student Advisory Council

Results of Rules Committee

Rules:

Priority:*

1. No sticking hands or head out of the window
2. No pushing out emergency window
3. No destroying property
4. No bothering, hurting, or embarrassing children or the bus driver
5. No fighting
6. No standing up when seats are available
7. No shouting

Consequences:

1. All children who ride the bus are expected to follow the rules. If they do not, these are the consequences:

   A. The bus driver will assign them to the front seat next to the door. They will board their bus last at their bus stop; get off the bus last at school and board the bus last at school to return home. The bus driver will decide how long this should continue. He will issue a ticket and give the ticket to Dr. Shaheen, or he will tell Dr. Shaheen and Dr. Shaheen will issue a ticket.

2. If a second ticket is issued to a child, the child's parents will be called by Dr. Shaheen. The child will be with Dr. Shaheen when the call is made.

3. If a third ticket is issued, the child will not be able to ride the bus for one week.

4. If a fourth ticket is issued, the child's parents, and Dr. Shaheen will meet to decide what must happen to the child's bus riding privilege.

Other: Only the bus driver may report children and issue tickets. There are no monitors who report people or who play police people.

---

*Note: The committee has prioritized the rules with number 1 being the most important and number 7 the least.

Figure 8-6

Blauvelt Elementary School

Student Advisory Council

Suggestions for Bus Drivers

1. The bus driver should report children who do bad things to Dr.Shaheen.
2. Bus driver should not yell so much—some children really get upset at yelling.
3. Bus drivers should be the same—not changed.
4. Bus drivers should drive carefully.
5. Bus drivers should not drive so fast.
6. Bus drivers should make sure that people stay in their seats.
7. The bus drivers should not ignore kids who do mean things.
8. The bus drivers should stop a noisy bus until it gets quiet.
9. The bus driver should not play with any child.
10. The bus driver should not favor certain kids.
11. No bus driver should bring candy on bus.
12. If bus is too crowded, should have two buses.
13. The buses should be clean and have seat belts.
14. The bus driver should be careful going around some bad curves—some kids get frightened.
15. Bus driver should stop kids from going wild.
16. Bus drivers should be consistent in what they do.

Figure 8–7

to elect two "bus trip observers"—one for each bus. These observers were given the task of evaluating the effectiveness of the program by reporting to Dr. Shaheen periodically whether or not the trips are safe and pleasant.

- The rules committee made posters for each classroom to display the rules.

Of course, it is not possible for us to say that SAC solved the bus problem—such problems have a way of being with us for all time. Nevertheless, pupil behavior on the bus, as evaluated by children, parents, and teachers, has improved markedly. The observers are reporting that almost all trips are both safe and pleasant.

Blauvelt Elementary School

February 12, 19——

TO: Bus Monitors

FROM: Little SAC

SUBJECT: Suggestions

Dear Bus Monitors:

Will you please help the people on the buses? After the kindergarten children get on the bus, why not let us on without waiting so long? We would like that.

Please also take care of the children who get hurt. If people are standing up and they fall down, would you try to take care of them?

Could you also not be so bossy? We don't like it when you say things like, "Sit down and don't get up and shut up!" We would like you not to act so cool.

We will help you if you don't act so big.

Sincerely, and wanting to help,

Little SAC

Figure 8-8

The children and the staff at Blauvelt have used their newly learned problem solving skills to solve other problems in addition to the bus problem. Recently they have completed two projects—one to define the rules of kickball (e.g., "Only the four captains can turn in a player for not obeying the rules") and one to improve the climate in the cafeteria. In addition, a recent complaint from Little SAC— that 3rd, 4th, and 5th graders can go outside after lunch but 1st and 2nd graders can't—has been handled. (Their request was denied but reasons for the rule were given).

Dr. Shaheen and the teachers agree that problems are important enough to have their attention and the attention of other authority figures when parents, teachers, and/or children believe that there is a problem. Further, when it is decided by SAC that a problem is important enough to be given attention, all persons of authority who have something to do with the problem solution are involved *with* the children, and Dr. Shaheen acts as the children's advocate and facilitator. Dr. Shaheen believes that citizenship education in America must teach children how to dissent within the law, how to approach authority, how to "win" and how to "fail." The Superintendent of Schools, the owner of the bus company, the Assistant Superintendents of Business, of Buildings and Grounds, and police officers have always agreed to meet with the children when requested to do so. In this way, the children learn how service people can help, how they are truly servants and not slaves, how they can be involved in decision-making which is beneficial to the children.

Dr. Shaheen and her staff work in many ways to help the students gain skills in persuading others, in winning, in handling rejections, and in approaching others with respect. Persistently, the children hear these messages: "If you have a complaint or suggestion, and it is important, put it in writing; don't catch me on the run—I can't handle that. And, if your communication looks important, I will read it and help you." (The little ones are encouraged to seek a volunteer secretary.)

In fact, to support and encourage sugestions and ideas, Dr. Shaheen and the teachers often volunteer to perform secretarial functions. Just as important, when a child is frustrated, angry, feeling persecuted, the message is, "Tell me in a way that I can hear you. I can't hear you when you shout at me and disrespect me as a person."

Dr. Shaheen believes that a key ingredient to high student morale and self-esteem at Blauvelt is the constant involvement of the children in activities to make their school better. Big and Little SAC serve as an important organizational tool to enable the children to participate in a well-structured manner. The result is that problem-solving has displaced mumbling, grumbling, and grousing.

8.03 Encouraging Children to Express Themselves

Blauvelt children are constantly encouraged to express their feelings about themselves, their teachers, their school, and their principal. Dr. Shaheen frequently receives letters from the children. Some, such as the one reproduced in Figure 8–9, contain suggestions for improving the school. Others, such as the one in Figure 8–10, simply express how the child feels or what he likes or dislikes. Frequently children are asked to write about things that are beautiful or things that make children happy. An example of this kind of writing is reproduced in Figure 8–11. Dr. Shaheen responds to all letters.

Dear Dr. Shaheen,

The thing I like best about our School is Gym Class and I wish we could have more of it. I also wish we could have more Math and Spelling. I also would like a little more resess my teacher wants more to.

(signature)

Figure 8-9

January 10, 1975

Dear Dr. Shaheen,

I like vacation, open recess, partys, fire drills, putting on plays, and playing games when my contract is done.

I don't like reading, math, music, health, library and soggy fields.

Your friend,

(signature)

Figure 8-10

Things that are beautiful

My mother thinks the most butiful thing in the world is:

Little babys just born

My father thinks the most butiful thing in the world is my mother

Figure 8-11

Her response may be in writing or it may be in the form of a personal visit to a child or to a class.

Children are also encouraged to come to the office or to talk to Dr. Shaheen as she moves around the building. She listens responsively and teaches her teachers to do the same. Dr. Shaheen says, "We are trying to get the kids to speak up in lots of ways because we can respect them only if we hear what they are saying. It is only when we respect the person that we can help him solve his problem."

8.04 Handling Referrals to the Office

When a child is referred to the office for discipline, his first task is to fill out a lengthy referral form. (See Appendix H.) This form asks the child what happened, how he felt at the time, and why he felt that way. It also asks him to identify possible alternatives to the action he had chosen and to make suggestions to the principal, teachers, and other children regarding how they should respond to what he has done.

After the child completes the form, he meets with Dr. Shaheen, the child's teacher and all others affected by the child's behavior and they discuss what happened. At this time all of those at the conference usually try to help the child understand his own feelings about his behavior and how his behavior has affected them. As a result of the conference Dr. Shaheen may follow one or more of the child's suggestions. The decision, however, regarding what the consequences of the child's behavior will be, will be made jointly by the child and the conference group. Every effort is made to define consequences which relate directly to the behavior. Dr. Shaheen does not try to protect the child from the consequences of his behavior. She does, however, try to help him understand the situation in which he finds himself.

In such sessions Dr. Shaheen does a lot of listening and responding in such a way that the child knows he is being understood. She then tries to help him solve his problems.

8.05 Teaching Children About Authority

Dr. Shaheen talks with the Blauvelt children a lot about different concepts of authority—structural or formal authority, authority by example, authority by experience, and authority by knowledge.

She defines formal authority as "the right to be heard and obeyed because of one's position." She feels that when we say we want children to obey authority we usually mean that we want them to obey formal authority. "That approach," says Dr. Shaheen, "is not going to work today. Besides it's a kind of authority I don't have any respect for so I have trouble teaching kids to respect it. I think people should earn loyalty."

Authority by example is defined as the respect which a person earns by his actions—by his providing models of behavior which others might profitably adapt. Authority by right of experience is defined as that authority a person earns because he has had a variety of experiences which are relevant to the situation. Authority by knowledge or expertise is defined as that authority a person earns by possessing information which others do not possess or by being able to accomplish tasks which others can't accomplish. Dr. Shaheen feels that authority by virtue of example, experience, or expertise gives us the right to be heard and respected.

Perhaps an example of an incident is the best way to show how Dr. Shaheen teaches this concept. She describes the incident as follows:[4]

> Some time ago Linda Winslow, our librarian, came to me and said that one of the fifth grade classes had just been terrible to her. She had told them that they were too noisy and that she couldn't stand it and and one of the boys had spoken up and said, "Yes, you *can* stand our noise—you're paid to do that."
>
> Well, Linda was really upset and said that for several weeks things hadn't been going right. She felt that she and the kids weren't together and that she felt like a failure. She felt that something should be done. I said that I'd be glad to go into the classroom with Linda and talk to the kids but I warned her that we would be risking a lot. "You know," I said, "if we go into the class we may hear the truth and you may not like what you hear."
>
> So Linda thought about it and then she said, "Look, I have to go— let's try it, it's better than not know what's going on."
>
> So we went into the classroom that afternoon. I said that I was there because I was concerned about some things that had been happening and that I wanted to give them a mini-lecture for about five minutes and then after that I'd like to hear from them. I said that I was specifically there because one of the people in that classroom had said to Linda that she was "*paid* to put up with anything the kids wanted to shout" and that I really didn't buy that.
>
> So I spoke to them briefly about authority. I told them that my husband had once told me that as a principal to remember that I was a *servant* of the public and not a slave. And I told them that in my opinion a servant is different from a slave because a servant helps, guides, and facilitates—I used all those words. And then I said that whether or not a servant should be respected depends on several things.
>
> And so I took those 5th graders through formal authority, authority

---

[4]Transcribed from a tape recording and reproduced with the permission of Mrs. Linda Winslow.

by example, authority by experience, and authority by knowledge and pulled from them examples.

Then I said, "Now, let's look at Mrs. Winslow. Does she deserve your respect just because she is the librarian in your school?" In response to the question I shared my own position with them that I didn't think that was enough and that furthermore, I didn't think *I* deserved their respect just because I was principal. I said that I believed they should start with respect towards me and towards the librarian but if we didn't earn it then we shouldn't expect to receive it.

Then I asked, "Is Mrs. Winslow a good model for you? Does she have that kind of authority?" And one after another the kids said, "Sure she's a good model. She's always friendly; she doesn't yell at us; she talks to us nice. She helps us find things." They went on with other examples.

And then I said, "What about experience?" And I asked, "Linda, are you a new librarian? How long have you been here?"

And she said that she'd been a librarian for five years.

And so I said to the class, "Does she *act* like she has experience?" And five or six kids all the way around the room said things like, "Sure—because when we ask her specifically for a book on horses she can find it for us," and, "When I'm stuck with the encyclopedia she can help me find what I'm looking for."

And then we went on to a discussion of authority by expertise and they gave similar examples.

Well, by this time Linda was about in tears because it was just a beautiful experience. And so when we were through I said, "OK kids, that's where it is—I think the remark was out of line and maybe you and Mrs. Winslow have something to go on."

Part of discipline I think is leveling with kids. A problem is a problem and you have to bring it out in the open before anyone can deal with it.

The result of this incident was four-fold:

1) The children learned an important lesson about the nature of authority, and because the lesson was relevant to a real-life situation it will be remembered for a long time.

2) Linda Winslow felt good because she had been helped with her problem and she had an opportunity to feel deeply the children's fondness and respect for her.

3) The children felt good because their opinions had been asked about the moral issues involved in the incident. They knew that they had been wrong and they knew why they had been wrong.

4) The behavior of the fifth grade children in the library improved remarkably.

8.06 Creating Activities to Provide Excitement for Children Within the School Setting

"School," says Dr. Shaheen, "needs to be an exciting place, and if we don't create excitement for children, they will create their own. Too often their own kind of excitement leads to discipline problems."

Dr. Shaheen feels strongly that a school should be a busy place where people feel that there is never enough time to do everything they want to do. In short, the school should provide "sanctioned excitement" for its children. Following are examples of the kinds of activities which have been planned by staff, parents, and children to add excitement to everyone's lives.

(1) The Read-a-thon. Held once a year, a read-a-thon is a day when everyone in the school reads and earns money from pledges by parents, neighbors, and extended family members. The last read-a-thon netted $1,109 which was spent by the librarian for books, tapes, prints and slides for the library-media center. The children elected representatives to work with the librarian as she selected the materials.

(2) Gifts for Seniors. Children made small gifts, then shared them with a senior citizens group in the community.

(3) Balloon Day. The children released 330 helium-filled balloons, each carrying a personal "We Care About . . . ." message. Responses from people who found the messages made exciting reading. (One child's sage comment: "What if our balloon reaches China? They won't be able to read what I care about.")

(4) Metric Week. The entire school engaged in metric measurement activities for a week. A carnival provided opportunities for children to measure everything and everyone in sight and offered a variety of metric games. At an assembly the "Average Blauvelt Metric Boy and Girl" were honored. Miss Valerie Malkus, a Blauvelt teacher, assumed responsibility for this project.

Many more similar activities, too numerous to describe, were also offered.

Some examples: A variety of enrichment assemblies sponsored by the PTA; a Saturday Fair featuring displays of children's work; a cookie-baking project to benefit the Heart Fund (heart-shaped cookies); fund raising for the Save the Children Foundation to continue the support of two children; and a project to study mass production in which assembly lines were organized to create sandwiches for lunch.

Activities such as these can be offered in any school. All you have to do is invite people to think up exciting activities and they will do so. The result is that everyone will enjoy school more and behavior problems will be reduced.

SUMMARY AND EVALUATION

Much more could be written about Jo Ann Shaheen and Blauvelt Elementary School. We could, for example, describe the thorough but highly personalized teacher evaluation system which helps teachers improve their own competencies and build their own self-esteem. We could describe the extensive involvement of parents in many phases of the school's operation and the unique ways parents are kept well-informed of the progress of their children. We could describe the intensive inservice program designed to help teachers learn the communications-opening and problem-solving skills needed in a school such as Blauvelt. We have, however, described Blauvelt thoroughly enough so that you can see how some of the suggestions in the various chapters of this book can be implemented.

In Chapters 2 and 3 we have suggested a variety of ways to shape up a school, ways to provide an orderly but nonoppressive environment so that projects can be launched to attack the causes of poor morale and discipline. Dr. Shaheen has done this with her insistence that the rules of the school be obeyed (e.g., the snowballing incident) and with her systematic but humane procedures for handling referrals.

In Chapter 6 we offered a wide variety of suggestions for involving pupils in the extra-curricular programs of the school. Dr. Shaheen has involved the Blauvelt children in school improvement by vitalizing her student council. She is teaching her staff and children how to use systematic problem-solving techniques to solve real school problems.

In Chapter 7 we described several programs for teaching morals and values. Blauvelt has not adopted any of these programs but morals and values are taught consistently as children are challenged to analyze the moral dilemmas they face in problem-solving. Blauvelt's librarian, Linda Winslow, can testify that the children are being taught in a very practical but dramatic manner to respect the rights of others.

Each spring the Blauvelt parents are asked to fill out a comprehensive questionnaire describing how they feel about their school. The latest questionnaire provides us with the following information:

(1) Parents feel overwhelmingly positive about the school. Over 250 comments were made by parents in response to several open-ended questions. Of those 250-plus comments, only three were negative. Most were enthusiastically positive. An example:

> The children act better. The halls are quiet now. Last year they were always full of kids running around. The children have more respect.

(2) Eighty-two percent of the K-2 parents and seventy-five percent of the 3–5 parents indicated that their children "almost always" liked school.

(3) In response to the question, "What does your child fear most in school?" 77% of the 3–5 parents responded "nothing." (Incidentally 5% of the parents said that their children feared the "big tests" most.)

At Blauvelt pupil achievement in basic skills is measured by Gates McGinitie reading tests, Metropolitan Achievement Tests in math, and by the New York State Pupil Evaluation Program (PEP). The results have been encouraging.

On the PEP achievement tests, for example, Blauvelt pupils are above average in achievement within the district. Before the program was started 38 percent of the third grade students tested in stanine 7, 8 or 9 in reading and 47 percent in mathematics. Since the program has been underway the proportion of third grade students scoring in stanines 7, 8 or 9 has risen to 68 percent in reading and 70 percent in mathematics.

As might be expected, the children have shown particularly strong gains in problem solving skills. Before the efforts in climate improvement, the median third grade score in the problem solving subtest was at the 66th percentile. This year the median score had risen to the 85th percentile.

Blauvelt children come to school from homes which are average in socio-economic level and they achieve only average scores on group I.Q. tests. Yet they excel in achievement in reading and arithmetic.

What has made the difference? Dr. Shaheen and her teachers feel that the humanistic climate plus the emphasis on practical problem-solving are the key determinants. Her comment:

In reading, to some extent, and in mathematics especially, we are wiping away the typical socio-economic predictors.

The Blauvelt children are disproving the popular theory that a humanistic climate is accompanied by a lowering of achievement. On the contrary, it is becoming increasingly clear that children perform best in a caring, nurturing, stimulating climate.

Discipline problems are disappearing at Blauvelt. A casual observer in the school's hallways might periodically see groups of children, ages 6–12, moving unsupervised to their art, music, P.E. class, special education activity, or library. There is no fuss, no running, no loud noise to interfere with classes in session. Pupils have been told that no one on the staff can afford the time to watch them as they go from place to place. They have also been told that they might lose the privilege of going to such activities if their behavior is not appropriate. So far no privileges have been rescinded.

Also, the school's lunchroom has quieted down. One custodian, newly assigned to Blauvelt, testifies that "there is less food and mess on the floor after the whole school here is finished with lunch than there is after one-fourth of the children in other schools."

Other staff members notice that children speak more respectfully to adults and to one another than they used to.

There is less fighting on the playground than there used to be and there are fewer referrals to the office—for whatever reason.

Much of Blauvelt's success story is, of course, attributable to the personality of the principal. Dr. Shaheen has unified the parents, staff, and children in the school because she knows what she is doing and is able to convince others that she is right. She is consistent. What she says one day will be emphasized on another day by an action she takes, a problem she helps someone solve, or a decision she makes. She recognizes in every way possible the strong competencies of each staff member.

We've already said that Blauvelt people write lots of letters to one another.

Perhaps the significance of what is happening in Blauvelt can best be described in this excerpt from a letter written to Jo Ann Shaheen by one of the teachers:

The clean-up campaign—ecology endeavor—or whatever—was really fun. But I must tell you a very touching thing that happened while we were picking up beer cans. We were in the back of the school and a group of kids started looking in the door window of the 3rd grade office corridor hall. You were standing by the Art Room. When the kids saw you, they called back to me that Dr. Shaheen was in the hall—only it wasn't the bland kind of reporting that goes, "We see the principal." They looked genuinely *pleased* that they discovered you. And I believe that is exactly what is happening. The kids are discovering that there is someone here who really cares about them—and so is the faculty and it is making a *great* difference.

References and Bibliography

These reference materials are readily available. We suggest that, if you have not already done so, you begin a library of such materials which can be used by individuals and task forces working to improve student behavior in your school.

Chapter 1

1. CKF Ltd. Editorial Staff, Robert Fox Chairman, *School Climate Improvement: A Challenge to the School Administrator,* 1975, Bloomington, Indiana, *Phi Delta Kappa,* paperback, 141 pp. (See Chapter 4 bibliography for annotation.)

Chapter 2

1. "Battling Telephone Bomb Threats with Operation B," *Nation's Schools,* March 1973, p. 43.

An article describing bomb threat policies and procedures in a Ypsilanti (Michigan) High School.

2. Bell, Raymond, "Alternatives for the Disruptive and Delinquent: New Systems or New Teachers?" NASSP *Bulletin* No. 391, May 1975, pp. 53–58.

Raymond Bell directs an experimental project to train teachers to work with disruptive students. His article describes delinquency patterns and identifies pitfalls to avoid in designing alternative programs. The second part of his article describes how crisis intervention teachers can be utilized in schools.

3. Bureau of Alcohol, Tobacco, and Firearms, Department of Treasury, "Bomb Threats and Search Techniques," U.S. Government Printing Office, Washington, D.C. 20402 (35 ¢), 15 pp.

This short pamphlet is a gold mine of information for the task force developing policies and procedures for handling bomb threats. Of special value are the suggestions for preparing for such threats. Detailed procedures for searching a building are also given.

4. Commission on Administrative Behaviors Supportive of Human Rights, *Phi Delta Kappan*, December 1974, pp. 236–242.

This article presents a sample student code which can serve as a resource for the committee developing or revising the code in your school.

5. De Cecco, John P., and Arlene Richards, "A Way Out of Anarchy—Civil War in the High School," *Psychology Today*, November 1975, pp. 51–55.

The authors, who are practicing social psychologists, analyze the causes of conflict in schools and suggest a structural negotiations process as a means of conflict resolution.

The article would be of value to any group in your school that is studying the causes of conflicts or clique structure. It is also helpful to any faculty member who might be in a position of mediating conflict.

6. Juillerat, Ernest E., Jr., "For Worried Districts: Here's Lots of Sensible Advice for Lasting Ways to Cut Down School Vandalism," *The American School Board Journal*, January 1974, pp. 64–69.

This article defines six basic steps for improving district security. The steps, if followed, will result in your district's having a well-planned, efficiently operated security program.

7. National School Public Relations Association, *Discipline Crisis in Schools: The Problem, Causes and Search for Solutions.* Education U.S.A. Special Report, The Association, 1801 North Moore Street, Arlington, VA 22209, $4.75, Pamphlet, 64 pp.

The report explores causes of the breakdown in discipline and discusses conflicting viewpoints about what should be done. A variety of solutions is suggested. (See annotation, Chapter 3, #10.)

8. National School Public Relations Association, *Violence and Vandalism— Current Trends in School Policies and Programs.* The Association, 1801 North Moore Street, Arlington, VA 22209, 1975. Pamphlet, 80 pp. (Single copy is $6.75. Enclose check with order.)

This pamphlet provides a wide variety of practical suggestions for reducing violence and vandalism in schools. The extent of the problem is also documented and causes are described. Specific programs in operation in school districts are described. An excellent basic resource for any group working on the reduction of crime and violence.

9. "Parents on Patrol," *Nations Schools*, March 1972, p. 28.

This brief article describes an NAACP-sponsored program organized to protect children from youth gangs who were accosting them and stealing their belongings and lunch money.

10. Riles, Wilson, "Report of Task Force on the Resolution of Conflict in the Schools," summarized in *California School Boards*, September 1974, pp. 5–30. (Annotation in footnotes section of Chapter 2.)

11. Schnabolk, Charles, "Safeguarding the School Against Vandalism and Violence," *Nation's Schools*, August 1974, pp. 31-34.

This article summarizes the pros and cons of various types of surveillance systems.

12. "Students on Patrol," *Nation's Schools and Colleges*, November 1974, pp. 24-25.

The article describes the activities of the Parkdale High School Student Security Advisory Committee. Students hold workshops, suggest solutions to problems, take part in simulations they might encounter on patrol, and actually patrol the building and campus.

13. "Vandalism," and sub-title, "$1.00 per ADA = Kid's Incentives," *Nation's Schools*, December 1973, pp. 31-37.

This article describes a variety of ideas for reducing vandalism in schools. Summarized is the South San Francisco plan for providing incentive grants to individual schools, ways to improve school design, an idea for improving discipline on school buses, suggestions for involving parents and other citizens in the reduction of vandalism, and descriptions of various electronic devices.

14. "Vandalism: Take Tempting Targets Out of Washrooms," *Nation's Schools*, August, 1973, pp. 44-45.

This brief article describes a number of ways to reduce the vulnerability of a building to vandalism.

15. "Violence in the Schools: Everybody Has Solutions. . . . ," *American School Board Journal*, January, 1975, pp. 27-37.

This article reports on an American School Board Journal's opinion survey regarding various proposed "solutions" to the violence in schools problem. Also included are several reports of successful practices such as the Cleveland program to reduce vandalism.

16. Zauner, Phyllis, "Trailer Dwellers Guard Against Vandals," *School Management*, February 1974, p. 27.

This brief article describes the Elk Grove (California) Unified School Districts Vandal Watch Project.

Chapter 3

1. *A Legal Memorandum*, newsletter published by the National Association of Secondary School Principals, The Association, 1904 Association Drive, Reston, VA 22091. Single copies, 50 cents.

In preparing Chapter 3, we drew on information provided in three of these newsletters, "Student Discipline—Suspension and Expulsion," June 75; "Hair and Dress Code: Update," January 76; and "Methods of Discipline:

What is Allowed," May 76. If you do not have these three, you should order them. They treat each subject thoroughly and accurately and they provide the administrator with specific suggestions. The writing is refreshingly free of legal jargon. The information is equally useful for elementary and secondary administrators.

2. Ackerly, Robert L. and Ivan B. Gluckman, *The Reasonable Exercise of Authority II,* 1976, National Association of Secondary School Principals, The Association, 1904 Association Drive, Reston, VA 22091, pamphlet, 32 pp., $3.00.

This pamphlet, prepared by two attorneys who are highly knowledgeable and experienced in school law, is indispensable to any administrator working with school discipline problems. The summaries of legal issues are brief and clear. Specific suggestions for handling discipline problems in a fair, reasonable, and legal manner are given. The suggestions apply equally to secondary and elementary schools.

3. "Bridging the Suspension Gap," an article in *Nation's Schools and Colleges,* March 1975, pp. 12–13.

This brief article describes the in-school suspension program of the Dade County, Florida schools.

4. Carrison, Muriel, Bryan Lindsey, and others, "The Perils of Behavior Mod," "Behavior Modification: Some Doubts and Dangers," and other articles in a "Pro and Con" section of *Phi Delta Kappan,* May 1973, pp. 593–601.

A good over-all description of what behavior mod is and some precautions regarding its general use by teachers.

5. Crane, Robert L., and Marjory Jacobson, "Adjusted Study, Low Cost Remediation and Adjustment," NASSP *Bulletin,* Vol. 60 No. 397, February 1976, pp. 1–8.

This article describes a program for helping pupils improve their achievement and behavior in the Webber Junior High School, Saginaw, Michigan. Pupils referred to the program spend two periods a week in the adjusted study room instead of attending the class in which they are experiencing difficulty.

6. Gartner, Alan, Mary Kohler, and Frank Reissman, *Children Teach Children: Learning by Teaching.* New York: Harper & Row Publishers, Inc., 1971, 180 pp. (See references for Chapter 7, #4 for annotation.)

7. Goldstein, William, and Edward Lovely, "A Compromise on the Smoking Dilemma," NASSP *Bulletin,* February 1974, pp. 22–26.

This article describes how a large (1,900) 10–12 high school successfully opened outdoor smoking areas for use by pupils.

8. Hoback, John, and Joseph Levanto, "The Problem of Attendance: Research Findings and Solutions," tape of a speech given at the NASSP Convention, Las Vegas, 1975. Tape available from NASSP, 1904 Association Drive, Reston, VA 22091.

In this presentation two principals present contrasting views on how attendance problems can be solved.

9. National Association of Secondary School Principals Survey, see summary in *Nation's Schools Report,* October 13, 1975, p. 4.

10. National Schools Public Relations Association, *Discipline Crisis in Schools,* 1973, The Association, 1801 North Moore Street, Arlington, VA 22209, 64 pp., pamphlet $4.75.

This special report of *Education U.S.A.* probes in detail the subject of discipline. The pamphlet contains much useful information regarding a variety of topics, including the causes of discipline problems, legal implications and restrictions, corporal punishment, the use of drugs to control behavior, and advice for parents and teachers. This pamphlet can serve as a basic resource to any group of individuals seriously considering ways to improve discipline in a school.

One section, entitled "One Cautious Solution: Drugs," pp. 48–55, summarizes the position of the American Academy of Pediatrics and HEW on the use of drugs to help hyperactive children. Valuable information, including the history of the use of drugs in schools, is provided.

11. "Ten Factors Relating to Student Absenteeism," National Association of Secondary School Principals, *Spotlight,* December 1975.

This brief article summarizes the findings of a study of "factors related to absenteeism." Your task force on attendance problems may want to do a similar study. (See Appendix B for more information regarding the Norwich Free Academy.)

12. "Sex Discrimination," Nation's Schools Report, Vol. 2, No. 1, January 5, 1976.

This brief article reprints the Title IX grievance procedures developed by Glendale Elementary School District #40, Glendale, AZ.

13. Skinner, John L., "Project: Self-Development—a Week at the Nunnery," *The Guidance Clinic,* Parker Publishing Company, West Nyack, NY, May 1976.

This article describes in detail the retreat program offered to 100 Parma, Ohio students. The program has helped drop-out-prone and disruptive students improve their behavior in school.

14. "With a Little Help from Your Friends," *Nation's Schools Report,* November 1973, pp. 40–42.

This article describes the Palo Alto peer counseling program in some detail. Specific suggestions are offered regarding how to organize such a program.

Chapter 4

1. Banville, Thomas, "23 Ways to Modify Behavior," *Instructor,* November 1974, p. 94.

An excellent list of suggestions for teachers to help them with classroom management. You might want to include such a list in your faculty handbook.

2. Dinkmeyer, Don, and Don Dinkmeyer, Jr., "Logical Consequences: A Key to the Reduction of Discipline Problems," *Phi Delta Kappan,* June 1976, pp. 664–666.

The theory of logical consequences outlined in this article holds that, within limits, we should permit children to experience the consequences of their own behavior. Discipline, then, is a process of helping people learn from their own mistakes. Pupils learn from "the reality of the social order" by making choices regarding their own behavior. The concept is explained more thoroughly in Dreikur's book, *A New Approach to Discipline.*

3. CFK Ltd. Editorial Staff, Robert Fox Chairman, *School Climate Improvement, A Challenge to the School Administrator,* 1975, Bloomington, Indiana, *Phi Delta Kappa,* pamphlet, 141 pp. ($3.00).

This book is a basic reference for any group or individual interested in improving school climate. The concept of school climate is carefully defined and instruments are suggested for its measurement. These instruments can be used to identify those components of a school's climate which are strong and those which are weak. This information can then be used by faculties or task forces to decide on the type of school improvement projects they wish to initiate. Progress can then be charted.

4. Glasser, William, "A New Look at Discipline," *Learning,* December 1974, pp. 6–11.

This article provides a brief introduction to Dr. Glasser's approach to discipline. Ten specific suggestions for improving discipline in the classroom are given.

5. Goble, Frank G., *The Third Force: The Psychology of Abraham Maslow.* New York: Grossman Publishers, Inc., 1970, 201 pp.

This book, written for the layman, describes Maslow's psychology in a direct, easy-to-read style. Of special interest to educators is Chapter 4 which describes Maslow's Theory of Basic Needs.

6. Grantham, Marvin L. and Clifton S. Harris, Jr., "A Faculty Trains Itself to Improve Student Discipline," *Phi Delta Kappan,* June 1976, pp. 661–663.

This article describes a successful staff development program in the Herbert Marcus Elementary School in Dallas.

7. Muuss, Rolf E., *First Aid in Social Situations, A Manual for Teachers.* Cleveland, Educational Research Council of America, 1968, 29 pp. (Available from the Council, Rockefeller Building, 4th floor, Cleveland, OH 44113.)

This brief document, together with Karen Todd's publication on promoting mental health will give the reader a working knowledge of the "causal approach to human behavior." The assumption behind this approach is that behavior is caused and that disruptive behavior can be changed if the cause of this behavior can be identified and treated. This manual defines the basic principles of the causal approach, then provides the teacher with a series of practical suggestions for applying those principles in the classroom. It is, to a large extent, a "how to do it" book for teachers who want to control behavior by understanding its causes.

8. Olivero, James L., *et al., Self Performance Achievement Record* (SPAR), a publication of CFK Ltd. and CADRE, Hillsborough, California, Nueva Learning Center, 1973.

This pamphlet describes in detail how teachers and administrators can use SPAR to directly relate an individual's self-improvement activities to actual school improvement projects. Available from the Nueva Learning Center, P.O. Box 1366, Burlingame, CA 94010, $3.50.

9. Palomares, Uvaldo H., and Terry Rubini, "Human Development in the Classroom," a chapter in Read and Simon's *Humanistic Education Sourcebook:* Englewood Cliffs, N.J.: Prentice-Hall, Inc., 1975, pp. 383–387.

This chapter summarizes the Human Development Program and the "Magic Circle" technique which teaches children self-awareness, self-confidence, and social interaction skills. Teachers need special training and materials to implement this concept. Once trained, however, the teacher can help his pupils control their own behavior by understanding themselves better. Training manuals and information regarding teacher training institutes are available from the Human Development Training Institute, El Cajon, CA.

10. Read, Donald, and Sidney B. Simon, *Humanistic Education Sourcebook,* Englewood Cliffs, N.J.: Prentice-Hall, Inc., 1975, 482 pp.

This sourcebook is a gold mine of material for anyone planning inservice activities for faculties interested in improving school morale and discipline. A wide variety of techniques and instruments which can be used immediately by teachers are described. The list of authors contributing chapters reads like "Who's Who" in humanistic education.

11. Rogers, Vincent R., and Bud Church, *Open Education: Critique and Assessment,* pamphlet, 1975, Washington, D.C., Association for Supervision and Curriculum Development, 109 pages.

This pamphlet defines open education and offers a variety of practical suggestions for organizing open education classrooms. Case studies document reasons for failure as well as reasons for success.

The summary of research is valuable for teachers who want to reassure parents that open education does not endanger pupil achievement. Emphasis is on elementary, not secondary, programs.

12. Schmuck, Richard A., and Patricia Schmuck, *A Humanistic Psychology of Education: Making the School Everybody's House,* Palo Alto, CA: Mayfield Publishing Co., 1974.

This book can serve as an excellent source book and text for any faculty group studying ways to improve discipline and morale in a school. A number of suggestions are offered for inservice activities and some specific suggestions are offered for improving the cohesion and over-all effectiveness of learning groups (Chapter 5).

13. Todd, Karen Rohne Pritchett, *Promoting Mental Health in the Classroom,* 1973, pamphlet, National Institute of Mental Health, 86 pp. (Available from U.S. Government Printing Office, Washington, DC 20402 for $1.25.)

This publication contains 13 units of study designed to be used in inservice programs for teachers. The units were designed by the author and psychologist Ralph H. Ojemann of the Educational Research Council of America. Units deal with such topics as motivation, principles of growth and development, managing classroom behavior, the teacher's behavior in the classroom, teaching about human behavior, and promoting self-directed learning.

Chapter 5

1. Bechtol, William M., *Individualizing Instruction and Keeping Your Sanity.* Chicago: Follett Publishing Co., 1973, 192 pp.

This book could well serve as a basic reference for any group of teachers desiring to individualize instruction. It is especially helpful to teachers seeking ways to manage such programs efficiently. Dr. Bechtol has had practical experience with all of the ideas he advocates.

2. Brown, B. Frank, *Education by Appointment: New Approaches to Independent Study.* West Nyack, N.Y.: Parker Publishing Company, 1968. 175 pp.

This book provides a large number of suggestions to educators wishing to initiate an independent study program. The rationale for independent study is convincingly given. The book then describes in detail how such programs should be designed and how they should function.

3. Brown, B. Frank, *The Nongraded High School.* Englewood Cliffs, N.J.: Prentice-Hall, Inc., 1963, 223 pages.

This book is as relevant today as it was when it was written. Dr. Brown describes how, through what he termed a "curriculum in motion" system, a school can get pupils excited about learning. At Dr. Brown's Melbourne High School the drop-out rate was lowered and student morale was improved. Discipline problems were rare.

4. Education Development Center, *Teacher and Classroom Involvement in an Alternative Approach to Large Scale Achievement Testing,* EDC Report, EDC, 55 Chapel Street, Newton, MA 02160.

A report on a million dollar project designed to develop criterion referenced tests related directly to pupils' learning activities.

5. "Alternatives to Grading." *Educational Leadership,* Journal of ASCD, Volume 32, No. 4, January 1975.

The entire issue of this authoritative national journal is devoted to articles concerning grading practices. This publication is a must for any committee or task force studying grading practices.

6. "News Front," *Education USA*, January 5, 1976, page 106.

A brief article reporting NEA's position on standardized testing. NEA objects to such tests on many of the same grounds as have been noted in this chapter.

7. Glasser, William, *Schools Without Failure*. New York, Harper & Row Publishers, Inc., 1969.

Glasser describes graphically how schools cause failure and makes suggestions for preventing failure.

8. Glines, Don E., *Creating Humane Schools*. Mankato, Minnesota: Campus Publishers, 400 pp.

This book describes the wide variety of innovations under way in the Wilson Campus School, a school which has combined a wide variety of innovations into the nongraded structure.

9. Hawes, Gene R., "Testing, Evaluation, and Accountability—Managing Open Education," *The Nation's Schools*, June 1974, Volume 93, No. 6, pp. 33-47.

This article provides nine examples of techniques for evaluating pupil performance which can be substituted for standardized testing.

10. Holt, John, *The Underachieving School*. New York, Dell Publishing Co., 1969, 207 pp.

John Holt is one of the best known and most outspoken critics of today's schools. One section of this book is devoted to criticisms of testing programs.

11. Howard, Eugene R., "How to Organize a Non-Graded School," Chapter 5 in *Handbook of Successful School Administration*. Englewood Cliffs, N.J.: Prentice-Hall, Inc., 1974, 696 pp.

This chapter describes how two schools, one elementary and one high school, have been organized for nongradedness. Specific programs within each school are described and steps for moving from a graded to a nongraded structure are defined.

12. Kinghorn, Jon Rye, "Individually Guided Education: A High School Change Program," NASSP *Bulletin*, March 1974, pp. 24-29.

Jon Kinghorn, as director of I/D/E/A's efforts to disseminate the IGE concept, is one of the country's most knowledgeable experts on IGE. In this article he describes the IGE model for high schools and emphasizes IGE as a change process. The article provides a good, brief introduction to the concept for those who may not be familiar with it.

13. Kirschenbaum, Howard, Sidney B. Simon, and Rodney W. Napier, *Wad-Ja-Get? The Grading Game in American Education*. New York: The Hart Publishing Company, 1971, 315 pp.

This book, available in paperback, provides an excellent summary of research on grading practices and a list of alternatives to letter grading. It is written in narrative form, free of educational jargon. It is an excellent primary resource for any individual or committee studying a school's grading practices.

14. Klausmier, Herbert J., *et al, Individually Guided Education in the Multiunit Elementary School,* 1969, Madison, Wisconsin, Wisconsin Research and Development Center for Cognitive Learning.

This is one of several basic references describing how to implement an IGE program in an elementary school.

15. Martin, Margaret, and Burrows, Charlotte, "Louisiana's High Flying Apollo School," pp. 4-9, *American Education,* March 1973.

This article describes how Apollo, a nongraded demonstration school, is organized for "continuous progress" instruction. The school has few discipline problems even though 700 pupils work together in one large open area.

16. Meier, Deborah, *Notes from City College Advisory Service to Open Corridors,* March, 1972.

A very thoughtful article detailing why standardized reading tests are harmful to the learning process. Copies no longer generally available.

17. "Math Study Slams Standardized Tests," *Nation's Schools Report,* December 8, 1975, Volume 1, No. 6.

This article summarizes the report of the National Advisory Committee on Mathematics Education (NACOME) regarding standardized testing.

18. Olivero, James L., *Chicken Little Was Right or The Future of Education Is Now,* Sioux Falls, S.D.: Adept Press, Inc., 1975, 138 pp. (paperback).

This book, written by the director of the Nueva Learning Center, describes a variety of ideas which the center demonstrates and promotes. It is an excellent resource for task forces working to modify the climate of a school.

19. Popham, James W., "Appropriate Assessment Devices for Educational Evaluation," a presentation at the *National Forum on Educational Accountability,* Denver, Colorado, May 8-9, 6 pages.

This paper is an excellent resource for any task force developing an evaluation program for a school. Popham, a recognized expert in testing, cautions educators against the misuse of various types of tests. Copies are available from Eugene R. Howard, Director, Accreditation and Accountability Services Unit, Colorado Department of Education, 201 East Colfax, Denver, CO 80203. Send 50¢ for reproduction costs and postage.

For more detailed information see Popham's book *Educational Evaluation.* Englewood Cliffs, N.J.: Prentice-Hall, Inc., 1975.

20. Purkey, William W., *Self-Concept and School Achievement.* Englewood Cliffs, N.J.: Prentice-Hall, Inc., 1970, paperback, 86 pp.

Dr. Purkey's book is a valuable resource to any group working to upgrade pupils' self concepts. Such groups are sometimes accused of "neglecting the basics." This book cites convincing research which shows that achievement is to a large extent determined by how a pupil perceives himself.

21. Simon, Sidney B. and James A. Bellanca, *Degrading the Grading Myths: A Primer of Alternatives to Grades and Marks,* 1976, Washington, D.C., Association for Supervision and Curriculum Development (ASCD), 151 pp., $6.00.

   This pamphlet, prepared in cooperation with the National Center for Grading/Learning Alternatives, reports on the research regarding commonly used grading practices and suggests a variety of alternatives to such practices.

22. Simpson, Sister Mary, "Rank in Class: An Educational Evil," *North Central Association Quarterly,* Spring, 1972.

   This article should be required reading for members of any group studying grading and ranking practices. The article provides a sound rationale for humanizing grading and ranking practices.

Chapter 6

1. Hartman, Rose Ann H., "Volunteerism in the Volunteer State," *Phi Delta Kappan,* Vol. LVI, No. 9, May 1975, pp. 608-609.

   This article describes the student volunteer program in the Roane County (Tennessee) Schools and elsewhere. It also suggests a variety of sources for information regarding such programs.

2. Leonard, George, *The Ultimate Athlete.* New York: Viking Press, Inc., 1975.

   This book is a valuable source of new ideas for task forces seeking ways to vitalize physical education, intramural and athletic programs. Leonard is a critic of overemphasis in schools on competition and win-lose activities. He advocates a variety of new, experimental games, "movement education," expansion of recreational and lifetime sports.

3. Stephenson, Ross, "Half of Student Body Can Serve as Representatives," *Bulletin,* National Association of Secondary School Principals, Vol. 60, No. 396, January 1976, pp. 113-114.

   A brief article describing the organization of the Springport (Michigan) Middle School's student council.

4. Taylor, John, "Intromurals: A Program for Everyone," *Journal of Health, Physical Education and Recreation* (JOHPER), September, 1973, pp. 44-45.

   A brief article summarizing the University of San Francisco's new intromural program which is based on many new concepts of physical education, sports, and recreational activities,

Chapter 7

1. Bechtol, William, *Individualizing Instruction and Keeping Your Sanity.* Chicago: Follett Publishing Co., 1973.

   For annotation see bibliography for Chapter 5.

2. Brown, B. Frank, *Education by Appointment: New Approaches to Independent Study.* West Nyack, N.Y.: Parker Publishing Company, 1968, 175 pp. (For annotation, see bibliography for Chapter 5.)

3. Fantini, Mario D., *Public Schools of Choice: A Plan for the Reform of American Education.* New York: Simon and Schuster, Inc., 1973.

   This book offers the most comprehensive treatment available on the development and potential of optional public schools. The Berkeley, California plan, among others, is described. This book may be considered a basic text for any group planning alternative programs as a way of reducing behavior problems.

4. Gartner, Alan, Mary Kohler, and Frank Reissman, *Children Teach Children: Learning by Teaching.* New York: Harper & Row Publishers, Inc., 1971, 180 pp.

   This book describes a number of current learning-by-teaching projects and gives suggestions for designing such projects. Successful practices are described in detail and evaluation information from several programs is summarized.

5. "Gifted and Underachievers Draft Own Projects," NASSP *Spotlight,* December 1975.

   This brief article describes an independent study program which has been popular with underachievers as well as with successful pupils.

6. Harris, Thomas A., *I'm OK—You're OK, A Practical Guide to Transactional Analysis.* New York: Harper & Row Publishers, Inc., 1969, 278 pp.

   Dr. Harris, a psychiatrist, describes how both children and adults can be taught to analyze their own communications with others. In the process individuals learn how to control their own behavior.

7. Kapfer, Philip G., and Miriam B., eds., *Learning Packages in American Education.* Englewood Cliffs, N.J.: Educational Technology Publications, Inc., 1972, 233 pp.

   This book is one of the most comprehensive resources we know regarding learning packages. Of special interest to faculties in the early stages of implementing this concept are Chapter 2 on the *Unipac* and Chapter 3, entitled "The Single Page Learning Model."

8. "Moving to Quarter System Quadruples Course Choices," a brief article in the NASSP *Spotlight,* Newsletter of the National Association of Secondary School Principals, November 1975.

   This brief article describes how course offerings were increased in Dundee, Illinois when the school district adopted the quarter system.

9. Nelsen, Ralph T., "Focus: An Alternative Model That Works," *Phi Delta Kappan,* Volume LVI, No. 9, May 1975, p. 361.

   This article briefly describes the FOCUS program, then reports on the evaluation of the program's five objectives. The program, operating as a school within a school, utilizes a variety of learning laboratories instead of conventional classrooms.

10. Olivero, James L., *Chicken Little Was Right or . . . . The Future of Education Is Now!* Sioux Falls, S.D.: Adept Press, 1975. 138 pp. (For annotation see listing under Chapter 6, No. 18.)

11. Rowe, John R., (Project Director), *The New Model Me,* a 9-12 curriculum for meeting modern problems, Educational Research Council of America, Rockefeller Building, Cleveland, Ohio 44113.

    This curriculum has been designed for use in small groups, mini-courses, and regular courses to teach pupils to assume progressively more control over their own behavior. Both individual and group activities are suggested. The materials were originally developed in the Lakewood (Ohio) School District under a USOE Title III grant. Information is available from Mr. John R. Rowe, Project Director, Curriculum for Meeting Modern Problems, Lakewood Board of Education, 1470 Warren Road, Lakewood OH 44107.

12. Smith, Robert L., and Garry R. Walz, eds., ERIC Counseling and Personnel Services Information Center, *Developing Students' Potentials,* published by Capitol Publications, Inc., Suite G-12, 2430 Pennsylvania Avenue, Washington, DC 20037, 102 pp.

    This report summarizes three well-known approaches to human development training and reports on research regarding their effectiveness. It is a useful reference for faculty members and discipline improvement committees considering human development training as a way of improving pupil behavior.

13. Superka, Douglas, *Values Education Sourcebook.* ERIC Clearinghouse for Social Studies, Social Science Education Consortium, 855 Broadway, Boulder, CO 80302, 1976, 259 pp., $10.95.

    This book summarizes a large number of programs which have been designed to teach beliefs and values to elementary and secondary pupils. It can serve as a basic reference book for any group charged with planning a values education program for your school.

14. Weinstein, Gerald, and Mario D. Fantini, eds., *Toward Humanistic Education: A Curriculum of Affect.* New York: Praeger Publishers, (111 Fourth Avenue, New York 10003), 1970, 227 pp.

    Whether or not you are interested in educational alternatives, this paperback offers a variety of suggestions for designing a curriculum which supports the growth of pupil's self concept and positive feelings about himself and others. Specific learning activities are described.

Chapter 8

1. Briggs, Dorothy, *Your Child's Self-Esteem: The Key to His Life.* Garden City, N.Y.: Doubleday & Company, Inc., 1970, 341 pp.

A practical book for parents and teachers who want to help children to grow in self-confidence, to become learners, and to find joy in their work and play. Dr. Briggs' many suggestions and techniques are based on a psychologically sound and workable formula—the child's view of him/herself. This is a HOW book that is truly inspiring.

2. Canfield, Jack and Harold Wells, *One Hundred Ways to Enhance Self Concepts in the Classroom: Handbook for Teachers and Parents.* Englewood Cliffs, N.J.: Prentice-Hall, Inc., 1976, 253 pp.

As the title implies, this book provides the teachers (and all educators) with stimulating, gentle, instantly useful, love-filled exercises, strategies, and activities for enhancing the positive self-concepts of children and adults. All of those people who work with children in and away from school, at the church, in the home, at camps, will find the methods proposed to help children to develop genuine self-esteem practical, vital, and growth promoting.

3. Coppersmith, Stanley, *Antecedents of Self-Esteem.* San Francisco: W. H. Freeman & Co., 1967.

While this doctoral dissertation on the self-esteem of a group of junior high school boys is academic reading, it is a must for those who plan to help youngsters to develop positive, realistic self-esteem. Read the conclusions listed at the end of each chapter.

4. Dinkmeyer, Don C., *Child Development: The Emerging Self.* Englewood Cliffs, N.J.: Prentice-Hall, Inc., 1965.

A basic book for teachers who wish to understand the foundations for effective humanistic education. Principles and their implications are laid out in practical ways for teachers.

5. Ginott, Haim G., *Between Parent and Child.* New York: Macmillan, 1965, (available in paperback from Avon Books, the Hearst Corporation, 959 Eighth Avenue, New York 10019), 252 pp.

This book, written by a well-known psychologist, offers parents concrete suggestions for communicating with children and for establishing a relationship of mutual responsibility, love, and respect. Illustrative dialogs between parent and child help make the book interesting and understandable. We suggest that you use this book as suggested reading for any series of workshops on self-esteem which involves parents.

6. Gordon, Thomas, *Parent Effectiveness Training: The No-Lose Program for Raising Responsible Children.* New York: Peter H. Wyden, 1970.

Replete with examples and strategies to help parents to develop skills required to foster effective human relationships with their children. Especially valuable to parents in helping their children to grow in self-respect are the aids to resolving conflicts in a spirit of mutual respect, in friendship, and in peace.

Appendix A (Chapter 1)

CLEVELAND HIGH SCHOOL
ACTION PLAN

CLEVELAND HIGH SCHOOL

5511 - 15th Avenue South

Seattle, Washington

William Maynard, Principal

Cleveland High School

Action Plan - (1st year)

William Maynard, Principal

Goals	*Objectives*	*Evaluation*
1. Provide a safe environment for kids	1.1 – Establish "principal's" communication committee representative of all clique groups.	1.1 – Meet once or more per week. Develop trust and communication.
	1.2 – Eliminate outsiders.	1.2 – Tally number of outsiders entering.
	1.3 – Establish "Getting It Together" student weekend conferences.	1.3 – Staff group leaders plan structured and instructional experiences.
	1.4 – Establish student/staff "Climate Committee."	1.4 – Minutes of meetings. Implement ideas.
	1.5 – Meet with militant ethnic community groups and try to enlist support.	
2. Improve the image of Cleveland with our students.	2.1 – Positive image workshop for football team.	2.1 – Schedule Fall
	2.2 – Establish Cleveland P. R. Committee—student/staff.	2.2 – Implement ideas
	2.3 – Meet with all student groups.	2.3 – Schedule and on demand.
	2.4 – Establish student grievance procedure.	2.4 – Implement

Cleveland High School (cont'd.)

3. Change the image of Cleveland in the eyes of the community.

2.5 – Reduce drop-out, absentee and suspension rates. Administration, staff, student task forces.

2.5 – Implement. Keep comparative records.

3.1 – Establish a Cleveland P. R. Committee–staff, students, parents, and community people with P. R. expertise.

3.1 – Establish committee–Meet– Develop plan–Implement.

3.2 – Three or more positive news-paper articles.

3.2 – Document.

3.3 – Two or more positive TV reports.

3.3 – Document.

3.4 – Weekly column in community newspaper.

3.4 – Document.

3.5 – Schedule various performances and/or demonstrations by Cleve-land students for fellow students.

3.5 – Document and evaluate student reaction.

Appendix B (Chapter 2)

Administrative Regulations for Mapleton's
Vandalism Reduction Program

Mapleton (Colorado) School District #1

591 East 80th Avenue

Denver, Colorado 80229

Dr. George DiTirro, Superintendent

MAPLETON SCHOOL DISTRICT #1

591 East 80th Avenue

Denver, Colorado

ADMINISTRATIVE REGULATION—VANDALISM

A. *Purpose*

This regulation is promulgated for the purpose of implementing plans to minimize the effects of vandalism on the instructional program and on the District budget.

1. *Vandalism Plan*

A Vandalism Plan for the District Junior High and Elementary schools is hereby established. Its major provisions will be as follows:

a. Each district Junior High and Elementary school will begin the academic year with an advance funding against projected vandalism repairs equal in dollars to one and one-half (1½) times its average daily attendance. For example, if a school has 500 students in ADA, the beginning allotment would be $750.00.

b. The principal of each Junior High and Elementary school, or his designated representative, will be responsible for the submission of a monthly report (SCHOOL VANDALISM REPORT #   ) detailing all of the repairs and/or replacements necessitated by vandalistic acts. Costs will be assigned by the Assistant Superintendent and the Director of Maintenance.

c. These monthly reports will be forwarded by the 5th day of each month to the Office of the Assistant Superintendent. They will *not* be sent to the Maintenance Department.

d. After the May report has been received in the Office of the Assistant Superintendent, vandalism costs for each school will be totaled. The dollars remaining in each school's vandalism funding is the amount that may be spent for *school improvement.*

NOTE: School improvement is defined as projects, equipment, supplies, etc. that contribute *materially* to the program of the school. Examples might be landscaping projects, audio-visual equipment, library books, out-door play equipment, etc. Exclusions (not eligible expenditures) might be parties, picnics, personal gifts, etc.

e. Expenditures from the remaining vandalism funds must be selected by the students. The selection may be made by the entire student body or by a student committee designated by the principal. The principal has the approval/veto power over the selections. His guidance is imperative.

f. *All* vandalism costs must be reported. These costs include, but are not limited to, glass breakage, fire losses, door and lock breakage, costs associated with break-ins and burglaries, equipment thefts or destruction, etc.

g. Costs of summer vandalism are non-deductible.

h. This plan does not relieve school authorities from the responsibility for apprehension and/or identification of those persons committing acts of vandalism within their schools. If apprehension is possible and successful, every attempt must be made to demand restitution for damage from the perpetrator or his parents. Any restitution made will cancel that portion of any deduction made from the fund.

i. *Accidental* breakage, i.e., windows, equipment, etc., will not fall within the definition of vandalism, and will, therefore, not be deducted from the fund.

j. The principal is solely responsible for determining which acts of destruction are *accidental* and which are *willful.* Willful acts will be those reported as vandalism.

k. Principals, teachers and other staff members are encouraged to utilize all means at their disposal to solicit the support of the students for the plan. Again, assemblies, newsletters, newspapers (student), posters, booster groups, etc, can be used to get the message to students.

1. Any person, student or non-student, apprehended in an act of vandalism will be reported immediately to the Director of Security, who will take whatever steps he deems necessary to secure restitution or initiate charges against the vandal.

m. The Board of Education has secured a traveling award to be given annually to that school that has experienced the smallest expenditure from its vandalism fund.

2. *Vandalism Repair*

a. Maintenance and custodial personnel shall make a concerted effort to erase the effects of vandalism as soon as possible, on the premise that a building showing signs of vandalism invites further destruction, just as a well-kept building discourages destructive acts.

b. Maintenance and custodial personnel are requested to keep the grounds as free as possible of rocks, bottles, and other missiles that can readily be used to break windows. Also, all bushes growing next to buildings should be kept well-trimmed so that persons cannot hide in these areas.

c. Where burglar alarms exist, principals and maintenance mechanics are to assure their constant good repair.

Appendix C (Chapter 4)

CLASSROOM CONTROL INDEX

Eugene R. Howard

Edward Brainard

Several items on this instrument originally appeared in a checklist developed for teachers in Jefferson County, Colorado, by Dr. Edward Brainard. Dr. Brainard reports that the checklist is especially helpful to beginning teachers who experience difficulty with classroom control. It has also been used successfully by experienced teachers who want to reduce discipline problems and improve classroom morale.

School Discipline Desk Book

Classroom Control Checklist (1)

This instrument is designed to help you, the teacher, locate your strengths and weaknesses in promoting a positive classroom climate. Please rate yourself on each of these items, first indicating how you perceive your own behavior, then indicating how you would like to be able to rate yourself. We usually do not perceive ourselves as others see us. Therefore you may wish to validate your perceptions with others. You may also wish to plan self-improvement or climate improvement activities in those areas in which the greatest discrepancy exists between what is and what should be:

	What Is:				What Should Be:			
	Almost Never	Occasionally	Frequently	Almost Always	Almost Never	Occasionally	Frequently	Almost Always
	1	2	3	4	1	2	3	4

I. Relationships with Students

1. I show affection for students by touching them.
2. I am optimistic and cheerful when talking with pupils.
3. I treat pupils fairly. For example, I do not play favorites or punish the entire class for the actions of a few.
4. I have a sense of humor and use it frequently in the classroom.
5. I listen carefully to pupils and help them with their problems.
6. I keep my temper.
7. I operate on the assumption that the pupil wants to do the right thing.
8. I trust my pupils and my pupils trust one another.
9. I use positive reinforcement instead of punishment.
10. I praise my students both individually and collectively. I am careful, however, that praise not be used to build a dependency relationship between pupils and myself.
11. I am available to students before and after school to help or just to talk.
12. I treat pupils as I would want to be treated.
13. I am perceived by my pupils as a real (not a phony) person. I do not act a role when I teach.
14. Pupils respect me because they know I care about them and because of my professional competence rather than because of my power and position.
15. I know each pupil and his parents as people.
16.
17.

II. Structuring and Managing the Classroom

	1	2	3	4		1	2	3	4

1. My classroom is cheerful and attractive.
2. Pupils are involved in the making of rules and are committed to enforcing them.
3. Classroom rules are simple, enforceable, clearly worded, and known by all pupils.
4. Pupils assume responsibility for assisting me in the management of the classroom.
5. My established routines for such activities as collecting papers and distributing materials function smoothly.
6. I use preventative discipline. That is, I attempt to recognize and identify problems before they develop.
7. While I take attendance or perform other routine tasks, pupils work in small groups or independently.
8. I understand the social interrelationships (clique structures) among pupils and use this knowledge in managing the classroom.
9. I use the theory of logical or natural consequences (teaching children to deal with the consequences of their acts) rather than imposed punishment or behavior modification.
10. I seek outside assistance (from counselors, administrators, social workers, etc.) when I need help in improving my classroom management.
11. I use grades and other evaluative devices to increase each student's self-esteem rather than to decrease it.
12. The time schedule in my classroom is flexible.
13. In my classroom we use group problem solving techniques to solve management problems.
14.
15.

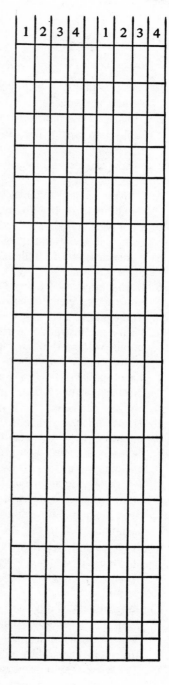

	1	2	3	4		1	2	3	4

III. Instructional Techniques

1. I involve pupils in planning and evaluating learning activities.
2. I manage classroom discussions so that all pupils participate. Discussions are orderly but lively.
3. I show sincere enthusiasm for the subjects I teach.
4. I insist on all students maintaining high standards in their work and their behavior but my standards are realistic for the age group and are attainable by all students.
5. I am successful in building the self-esteem of each pupil.
6. During supervised study I move about the room giving encouragement and assistance to the pupils.
7. I vary my instructional techniques so that pupils with varying learning styles (e.g., active, creative, visual) can benefit.
8. Each pupil in my class can identify at least one successful learning experience he has enjoyed each day.
9. I individualize assignments—i.e. all pupils are not assigned the same tasks.
10. I teach students how to study so that assignments are effectively completed.
11. I seek outside assistance (from counselors, administrators, social workers, etc.) when I need help in improving my instructional techniques.
12. I am patient with my pupils. I am willing to reteach without resentment concepts which were not understood when first presented.
13. Independent study and student-initiated projects are encouraged in my class.
14. The work that I assign is perceived as useful and meaningful by all my pupils.
15. The work that I assign is within the power of all students, provided they make the necessary effort.

	1	2	3	4		1	2	3	4

16. Before assigning work I use pre-tests and other diagnostic procedures to ascertain what pupils already know and can do.
17. I give directions one step at a time. I avoid long and detailed directions.
18. I use the "Magic Circle," "class meetings," or other discussion techniques to open communications in the classroom.
19. I use the chalkboard and other visual aids to present and review concepts and directions.
20. I sub-group pupils in such a way that all pupils grow in self-esteem (i.e. there is no stigma attached to any of the sub-groups).
21.
22.

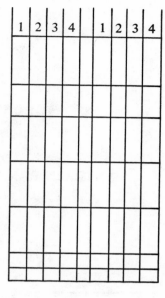

Appendix D (Chapter 6)

EXTRA-CURRICULAR ACTIVITIES CHECK LIST

Eugene R. Howard

SCHOOL DISCIPLINE DESK BOOK

Extra-Curricular Activities Check List

☐ Student　　　　　　　☐ Parent　　Date:_____

☐ Faculty Member　　　　☐ Administrator

This check list provides you with an opportunity for making suggestions regarding possible ways we might expand the participation of pupils in our extra-curricular programs.

Prior to completing the check list you should become familiar with the definitions of all of the terms. You may do this by attending a meeting called for that purpose or by reading Chapter 6 in the book, *School Discipline Desk Book*. One objective in increasing students' involvement in our activity programs is to improve student morale and thereby reduce discipline problems.

Please use an *X* to indicate the response which most nearly expresses your opinion. Do not sign your name. Your responses are confidential.

Items 17 and 18 are blank so that you can write in your own suggestions for improving participation in our activities programs.

When you have completed the check list please answer the questions at the bottom of the page.

IN THIS SCHOOL WE SHOULD	Strongly Agree	Agree	Disagree	Strongly Disagree
	1	2	3	4
1. Form a "Committee to Involve the Uninvolved."				
2. Open our student government to broader participation.				
3. Schedule more activities within the school day.				
4. Reduce "Hidden Tuition Costs."				
5. Operate a "late bus."				
6. Expand student service activities.				
7. Encourage the formation of more than one newspaper or magazine.				
8. Expand the membership on the cheerleader and pompon squads.				
9. Remove good scholarship as a requirement for participation in the Activities Program.				
10. Expand the intramurals program into an intromural program.				
11. Initiate a "no cut" policy in athletics (i.e., programs are open to all who wish to participate).				
12. Organize activities to enhance ethnic pride and awareness.				
13. Expand musical and dramatics activities.				
14. Increase the number and expand the variety of assemblies.				
15. Expand and modify the school's social programs.				
16. Organize programs to promote more friendliness among pupils and between pupils and staff members.				
17.				
18.				

QUESTIONS

1. Please list the two main reasons why more students do not participate in our extra-curricular activities.

2. Would you be willing to serve on a task force to improve student participation in our activities program? (If so, please sign the sign-up sheet.)

Appendix E (Chapter 7)

LEAL ELEMENTARY SCHOOL OPTIONS PROGRAM

Leal School

312 West Oregon

Urbana, Illinois 61801

Richard Bodine, Principal

Urbana School District 116

Urbana, Illinois

LEAL SCHOOL

Description of Options*

Basic Beliefs

Leal School provides three different approaches to teaching and learning at each grade level. We provide these "options" with full realization that there will be and must be great similarities of purpose through all the "options." We submit the following six basic beliefs common to all "options":

a. A quality education can be obtained through a number of alternative methods or programs (options). No one of the "options" is objectively better than another though different students may respond better to one "option" than another.

*This material originally appeared in a memorandum to Leal School parents from Richard Bodine, Principal.

b. Teachers are individuals and some feel more comfortable and successful working in one "option" rather than another.

c. All "options" should give attention to the basic skills.

d. All "options" must have instructional activities tailored individually to fit the needs of each student.

e. All "options" should provide an intrinsically satisfying experience in which learning is an enjoyable activity.

f. All "options" will work toward helping each student develop a more positive self-concept and a feeling of self worth.

Whereas the above listed beliefs represent the similarities among the "options," the following descriptive statements should serve to indicate some of the differences.

Option A

- Serves children of all abilities who want and need the security of structure. Also serves the child who, while not needing the structure, will accept it and function within it.

- Teacher has the primary responsibility for making decisions about subject matter goals and the use of time.

- Generally, the majority of students work on language arts and math at the same time. Grouping is flexible, depending on the varying needs of children and teachers. Both large and small groups are used for instructional purposes.

- Materials are primarily teacher chosen and of a great variety. System adopted texts, supplementary materials, and teacher made items are all used. These materials enhance the variety of activities, projects, and areas of study that are covered during the year.

- Within the structure, the wants and needs of children are treated on an individual basis both academically and socially. Teachers will have differing expectations and requirements. Each child is encouraged and challenged to better his or her own past performance.

- The physical appearance of the classroom will depend on the needs of students, teachers, and the subject being taught. While teachers of Option A attempt to adhere to the principles of the option, their individual styles of teaching and the age level of children will reflect some differences.

- Option A strives to involve the student in his or her own learning. This involves helping the student accept and develop responsibility for his or her actions and work. Children are helped to develop responsible work and study habits. Increasingly, as the year passes, children are helped to learn to budget their time wisely.

- Classrooms are essentially self-contained, with possibly some limited team teaching, with children of one or two age levels.

Option B

- Serves children of all abilities who want or need freedom, but within the security of an essentially self-contained classroom.
- Teacher has the primary responsibility for determining the objectives for the day to day operation of the program. The emphasis of Option B is to gradually encourage children to become independent learners. As the year progresses children receive increased responsibility in managing their time and materials. To varying degrees children make decisions concerning the manner in which they will carry out the objectives of the program. When given assignments, children are often encouraged to suggest alternatives which appeal to them. At other times, the teacher may suggest several possible projects or assignments which meet the requirements and the children must choose.
- Realizing that each classroom contains children of varying strengths and weaknesses, the teacher will have different expectations and requirements for each child. Each child is encouraged to better his or her own past performance.
- Materials are drawn from a variety of sources. In some areas a multi-text approach is used. Activity cards, worksheets, activities, projects, educational games, and library books are also considered an important part of the "option."
- The physical appearance of the classroom is determined by the needs of the children and teacher. An informal atmosphere usually prevails with a balance of quiet and more active times found in most classes each day.
- Grouping is flexible and is often based on interest as well as ability. Both large group and small group instruction activities are utilized with the emphasis on small group instruction and individual student-teacher conferences for follow-up and evaluation.
- Children are generally required to work on a variety of subjects each day. A child who is working in an area of special interest may be allowed to spend extended time on that topic. After required work is completed, children are expected to use their time wisely. Children should begin to challenge themselves to learn more about areas which interest them. Either the child explores this area of interest or follows through on a suggestion offered by the teacher. These challenges should be considered as an important part of the program.
- Children will increasingly learn to plan their own schedules by the day or week. They will develop skills of self-direction and time management.

- Classrooms are essentially self-contained, with possibly some limited team teaching, with children of one or two age levels.

Option C

- Serves children of all abilities with the potential to be self-motivated and who want to take the responsibility for his/her own learning. The child should like to move around and should be tolerant of others moving around. He or she should be able to concentrate despite a large variety of active learning activities and movement in the classroom.

- Students will be responsible for planning at least one-half of his/her time. The student will have the responsibility for choosing what he/she will work on, when he/she will work, and where he/she will work. Much of the time, children will choose what to study based on their interests.

- A strong emphasis is put on one-to-one guidance and small group work. Class meetings are held to plan, share ideas, solve group problems, and hear directions.

- A variety of activities in all subject areas will occur at the same time. Children will move toward assuming more responsibility for their own time and learning. Some assignments are required, especially in the areas of language and math.

- Teachers choose some of what they teach based on personal interests. Teachers encourage suggestions from children and carry them out when possible.

- Textbooks are utilized as resources and for guided instruction when applicable. Learning centers are developed to present ideas to students. A strong attempt is made to use community resources. Many teacher made units will be used as will manipulatives and equipment.

- All subjects utilize flexible groupings based on children's interests. Some math and language activities are skill grouped. Age is not considered in any grouping, although personalities and friendships may be.

- Option C is based on the following assumptions about learning and knowledge: no set curriculum is followed, children learn best where they are interested, children vary in the types of skills and subject matter they need, individuals vary in learning style thus varied approaches must be used in presentations, and children learn best when they develop a caring relationship with their teacher and their peers and activities are planned to promote this.

- Classrooms contain children of three age levels. Classrooms are grouped in clusters of three and each child has access to all three. Various rooms will be organized according to subject matter and materials. Furnishings will be informal and children and teachers will decide on the room arrangement and decor. Team teaching and the development of teacher specialties will be an integral part of the program.

These descriptions show that programs of the various options will provide variety at each age level. It must also be noted that variations will occur within the same option from age level to age level. Much of that variation is due to the maturity level of the students.

Appendix F (Chapter 7)

Summary of Available Values Education Materials

Dr. Larry L. Palmatier and Dr. Jon Davis

142 M. B. H.

University of Utah

Salt Lake City, Utah 84112

TABLE 1 INCULCATION PROGRAMS FOR STUDENTS

Character Education Curriculum	Freedom & Responsibility: A Question of Values	The Human Values Series
Objectives: 1) to inculcate honesty, generosity, kindness, tolerance, courage, responsibility, good citizenship 2) to attain sense of self-worth, develop decision-making and values clarification skills.	1) to clarify the concept of freedom and responsibility. 2) to direct students to the concept that accountability to self and society is proportional to one's freedom, and to the definition of freedom as "the opportunity to make choices within limits."	To inculcate key values consistent with the democratic view.
Content: in addition to (1) above . . . use of time and talents, freedom of choice, freedom of speech, the right to be an individual, to have economic security and equal opportunity.		Eight specific value categories - affection, respect, well-being, wealth, power, rectitude skills, and enlightenment.
Method: Open-ended use of teacher guide, posters, problem-solving, role playing, creative art.	Discussion questions, research activities, exercises.	Brief stories and pictures present issues and problems to students and end with a moral lesson.
Grade Levels: K–5	9-12	K-6

224

Table 1 (cont'd.)

	Character Education Curriculum	Freedom & Responsibility: A Question of Values	The Human Values Series
Materials and Costs:	Multi-media kit $16.95 per grade level	Audiovisual kit ($104.50) (slides, teacher's guide, student activity cards, cassettes or records)	$40.00 (student text, teacher's edition, eight large posters, teacher's kit)
Critique:	Program evaluation showed good to excellent results for earlier grades and strong rating by ASCA journal *Thrust* program and procedures.	No formal evaluation available although field testing is claimed by publisher.	Available from publisher. Some gain in reading and comprehension skills shown for upper grade students.
Publisher:	The American Institute for Character Education, 342 West Woodlawn, San Antonio, TX 78212 (P. O. Box 12617)	The Center for Humanities, Inc., Two Holland Ave., White Plains, NY 10603	Steck-Vaugh Company, P. O. Box 2028, Austin, TX 78767
Date:	1974	1973	1973

TABLE 2 INCULCATION PROGRAM FOR TEACHERS

	Becoming Aware of Values	Coronado Plan: Teacher's Guides	Human Value in the Classroom: Teaching for Personal and Social Growth
Author/Developer:	Bert K. Simpson	Marvin L. Bensley	Robert C. Hawley
Objectives:	the eight values of the Lasswell-Rucker framework.	1) to increase communication and self-awareness, improve self-image, understand the function and techniques of advertising and gain skills in decision-making and problem-solving. 2) to solve problems of drug abuse.	to achieve "social self-actualization"
Content:	Values of affection, respect, skill, enlightenment, influence, wealth, well-being, and responsibility.	Values of Lasswell-Rucker framework.	love, trust, interdependence, dignity, joy, community-building.
Method:	Six games, many exercises, worksheets, diary, reading, discussing.	reading, writing, discussion, and action projects related to subject matter.	group discussions, exercises in cooperation, specific lesson plans, communication techniques.
Grade Levels:	K–12	K–12	K–12
Materials and Cost:	$4.95 (Teacher's Guide)	$10.95 - Five books (teacher's guides and advertising guide)	$3.75 (Teacher's guide)

Table 2 (cont'd.)

Becoming Aware of Values	Coronado Plan: Teacher's Guides	Human Value in the Classroom: Teaching for Personal and Social Growth
Critique: The guidebook contains helpful sections-guidelines for administrators, four evaluation instruments, research references and review of children's books and the eight values	Extensive studies have been done on this program with many favorable results cited.	Evaluation instruments for rating teacher's openness are included in the guide and a practical treatment of grading, discipline, creative thinking and values concludes the book.
Publisher: Pennant Educational Materials, 4680 Alvarado Canyon Road, San Diego, CA 92120	Pennant Educational Materials, 4680 Alvarado Canyon Road, San Diego, CA 92120	Education Research Associates, Box 767, Amherst, MA 01022
Date: 1973	1974	1973

TABLE 3 MORAL DEVELOPMENT, STUDENT PROGRAMS

	First Things: Values	Holt Social Studies Curriculum	Moral Reasoning: The Value of Life
Author/Developer:	Lawrence Kohlberg and Robert Selman	Edwin Fenton	Alan Lockwood
Objective:	to help elementary students reason about moral issues.	1) to improve students' independent thinking abilities and to clarify their responsibilities as citizens. 2) develop a better attitude toward learning, acquire a positive self-concept, value, develop learning skills, develop inquiry skills, and attain knowledge.	to help students formulate, clarify and justify their thinking about the value of life.
Content:	Open-ended dilemmas on such topics as keeping promises, telling the truth, respecting property rights, sharing, understanding the reasons for rules.	Seven courses (Comparative Political Systems, Economic Systems, The Shaping of Western Society, Tradition and Change in Four Societies, A New History of the United States, The Humanities in Three Cities, Introduction to the Behavioral Sciences.)	The value of life in the context of conflict with such values as obedience to law, political and familial loyalties, and cultural diversity.
Method:	Spontaneous discussion of moral issues in dilemmas.	Students' readings and class discussions, other activities based on Kohlberg's moral reasoning about dilemmas.	discussions of moral dilemmas.

228

Table 3 (cont'd.)

	First Things: Values	Holt Social Studies Curriculum	Moral Reasoning: The Value of Life
Grade Levels:	1-5	9-12	9-12
Materials and Cost:	$ 19.50 - six audiovisual kits with film-strips $ 21.50 - teacher's guide and records or cassette tapes.	$ 5.00 - $ 9.00 each student text $ 3.00 - $ 5.00 each teacher's guide $112.00 - $ 180.00 - multi-media kit of film-strips, records, class handouts, exercises, readings, transparencies, testing program, teacher-training filmstrip.	$ .50 (each student text; teacher's guide free with purchase of ten or more student books).
Critique:	Instruments for evaluating students' progress are not included in the program but field testing of the program itself appears to be comprehensive and very favorable.	Materials are strong in the area of inquiry skills development and require much reading by students.	No program evaluation is available. Internally there are student evaluation materials.
Publisher:	Guidance Associates, 757 Third Avenue, New York, NY 10017	Holt, Rinehart and Winston, Inc., 383 Madison Avenue, New York, NY 10017	Xerox Education Publications, Education Center, Columbus, OH 43216
Date:	1972	1969-75	1972

TABLE 4 MORAL DEVELOPMENT, TEACHER PROGRAMS

Getting It Together: Dilemmas for the Classroom

Author/Developer: Beverly A. Mattox
Publisher: Pennant Educational Materials
4680 Alvarada Canyon Road
San Diego, CA 92120

Date: 1975

Grade Levels: 1-12

Materials and Cost: Teacher's Guide ($ 3.95)

Objectives: to provide teachers and administrators with an understanding of Kohlberg's moral development approach to values education and practical skills for implementing this approach.

Content: Kohlberg's theory, including the stages of moral development, teaching techniques, classroom climate, 45 classroom dilemmas and steps for writing dilemmas oneself.

Method: Dilemma, discussion, simulation, role play.

Critique: This book is a fine resource for anyone wishing a concise introduction to Kohlberg's model.

A Strategy for Teaching Values

Thomas Lickonia, with Lawrence Kohlberg and Robert Selman
Guidance Associates
757 Third Avenue
New York, NY 10017

1972

1-5

$ 19.00 - $ 21.50 Audiovisual kit (guide, filmstrips, records or cassettes)

to help teachers use effectively the student program, FIRST THINGS: VALUES series (described in Table 3).

Kohlberg's theory and methods of applying the theory of moral development to the classroom.

small group discussions, filmstrips.

This is a good simple introduction to Kohlberg's model and teaching methods.

TABLE 5 ANALYSIS, STUDENT PROGRAMS

American Values Series: Challenges and Choices	Analysis of Public Issues Program
Author/Developer: Jack L. Nelson, Editor Publisher: Hayden Book Company, Inc. 50 Essex Street Rochelle Park, NJ 07662	James P. Shaver and A. Guy Larkins Houghton Mifflin Company 1 Beacon Street Boston, MA 02107
Date: 1974–75	1973
Grade Levels: 9-12	9-12
Materials and Cost: $ 2.00 average per book	Student text ($ 5.00); teacher's guide ($9.00); audiovisual book; duplicating masters and problem booklets ($93.00).
Objectives: to encourage students to develop a questioning attitude toward social issues and to make decisions based on facts, value analysis, and projected consequences.	to foster in students the skills to analyze critically controversial public (ethical) issues.
Content: The series consists of seven books on contemporary American problems (Rights of Women, The Environment, War, City Life, Urban Growth, Values and Society, Value Inquiry and Values and Society)	right to representation vs. respect for authority, unreasonable laws vs. respect for law, law and order vs. equality, friendship vs. mercy killing.
Methods: Case studies, data banks, discussion, community involvement, futuristic scenarios.	case studies and value dilemma episodes both personal and social recitation, socratic and seminar.
Critique: No evaluation available.	No formal evaluaton of the program is available but the program does contain a test for measuring students' learning of the major value conflicts.

TABLE 6 ANALYSIS, TEACHER PROGRAMS

Title: Values Education–Rationale, Strategies, and Procedures

Author/Developer: Lawrence E. Metcalf

Publisher: National Council for the Social Studies, 1201 - 16th Street N.W., Washington, D.C. 20036

Date: 1971

Grade Levels: K–12

Materials and Cost: Teacher's Guide $ 5.00

Objectives: To help students: 1) Make rational value judgments.

2) Develop capabilities of making rational value decisions

3) Resolve value conflict between themselves and other members of a group.

Content: Definition of value judgments, teaching strategies for Value Analysis methods of resolving value conflicts, and many specific examples using real world value conflict.

Method: Step-by-step procedures for resolving value conflict are given, one an eight-step plan, the other a fourteen-step plan.

Critique: It would be nice and also convenient if the world's problems could be solved in six or eight or even fourteen logical steps. While things are not that simple the procedures in this program are helpful in giving a solid structure for one's decision-making.

TABLE 7 VALUES CLARIFICATION: STUDENTS' PROGRAMS

Decision-Making: Dealing with Crises and Deciding Right from Wrong: The Dilemma of Morality Today	Dimensions of Personality: Search for Meaning
Publisher: The Center for Humanities, Inc. Two Holland Avenue White Plains, NY 10603	**Authors:** Ronald Klein, Rose Marie Kramer, Romaine Owens, Mary Jane Simmons, and Karen Walsch **Publisher:** Pflaun Publishing, 2285 Arbor Blvd., Dayton, OH 45439
Date: 1974	1974
Grade Levels: 9-12	7-8
Materials and Costs: Audiovisual kit containing 160 slides, 2 tape cassettes or records, and teacher's guide ($100.00 per title).	Multi-media kit with teacher's guide, book of 71 spirit masters, and 12 posters ($ 45.00).
Objectives: to teach students decision-making and judgment-forming skills, crisis management and the origins of personal and social moral standards.	to help students examine their lives and clarify their values in external and internal forces and their relationships with others.
Content: Problems of drinking, pregnancy, school and home. Crucial historical and literary decisions and their personal and social consequences are examined.	capability, flexibility, growth, responsibility, relationships with family, friends, and the opposite sex.
Methods: Case studies, discussions, warm-up activities, and research activities.	warm-up discussions, self-analysis worksheets, writing, role playing or simulation.
Critique: This is an excellent and practical way to engage students in true to life values clarification experiences.	Material is reported to be relevant and discussions lively. At times students complain about the writing they must do on the self-analysis sheets.

TABLE 7 (cont'd.)

Making Sense of Our Lives	Meeting Yourself Halfway: 31 Value Clarification Strategies for Daily Living
Author: Merrill Harmin	Sidney B. Simon
Publisher: Argus Communications 7440 Natchez Avenue Niles, IL 60648	Argus Communications 7440 Natchez Avenue Niles IL 60648
Date: 1974	1974
Grade Levels: 7-12	7-12
Materials and Cost: Spirit masters, posters, teachers' suggestion sheets ($ 36.00 approx.)	Student/teacher book $ 4.95; with spirit masters $ 18.50.
Objectives: to help students discover meaning and direction in their lives to face complexity, to listen to others and to stand up for their beliefs.	to gain a level of self-discovery which helps one gain a clearer view of his identity and his values.
Content: problems of prisons, race, old age, the future, etc.	Activities include personal inventories, decision-making, considering priorities, risks and consequences, and taking action.
Methods: Value dilemmas are presented on cassettes. Readings, activities, discussions and play writing are also conducted.	A positive, self-affirming approach is used individually or in small groups.
Critique: The author tested his materials in workshops but no formal evaluative results are available.	Evaluation of the experiences is left to the individual.

TABLE 8 VALUES CLARIFICATION: TEACHERS' PROGRAMS

	Value Clarification in the Classroom: A Primer	Values Clarification: A Handbook of Practical Strategies for Teachers and Students
Authors:	J. Doyle Casteel and Robert J. Stahl	Sidney B. Simon, Leland W. Howe, and Howard Kirschenbaum
Publisher:	Goodyear Publishing Co., Inc. 15115 Sunset Blvd. Pacific Palisades, CA 90272	Hart Publishing Company 719 Broadway New York, NY 10003
Date:	1975	1972
Grade Levels:	9–12	K–12
Materials and Cost:	Teacher's Guide ($ 7.95)	Teacher's Guide ($ 3.95)
Objectives:	to help teachers organize and guide instruction in the area of values clarification so that students learn to analyze values, express themselves, empathize and solve problems.	to help teachers and students clarify their own values and behave more positively, purposefully and enthusiastically.
Content:	Four phases are followed - comprehensive reason, valuation and reflection, the clarification of values in government, history, anthropology, economics, population studies, etc.	Seventy-nine values clarification strategies ranging from sentence completion to rank ordering.
Method:	Value sheets are used in one of six formats - standard, forced-choice, affirmative, rank order, classification and criterion. Activities include readings, discussions, writings, and role play.	Completing self-analysis worksheets and discussing value positions in small groups are the primary activities.
Critique:	The program represents a detailed and well-organized framework applicable to practically every subject.	There is some evidence that students become less apathetic and flighty and become more vital and purposeful.

TABLE 9 ACTION LEARNING PROGRAM FOR STUDENTS

Title: Social Action–Dilemmas and Strategies (Public Issues Series)

Directors: Fred M. Newmann and Donald W. Oliver
Publisher: Xerox Education Publications, Education Center, Columbus, OH 43216
Date:. 1972
Grade Levels: 9–12
Materials and Cost: Student text ($.50) teacher's guide (free with 10 or more student
    books).
Objectives: to help students identify their own interests and raise questions about
    social action projects (legitimacy of involvement skills needed for
    effectiveness, strategies used, dilemmas faced and personal commitments
    needed). The purpose is not to get students involved in any particular
    social issue.
Content: Booklet of case studies of actual student involvement in social action.
    Social action is not radication, but is defined as any deliberate attempt
    to influence an institution or public policy.
Methods: Students read case studies of social action projects and discuss and role
    play their reactions. Other activities are research, field trips to community
    agencies, interviews of public officials, and surveys of community atti-
    tudes. If students find a cause they wish to pursue they are encouraged
    to draw up a plan of action and carry it through.
Critique: Parental and school support of action projects is not always forthcoming,
    so the book contains suggestions for gaining such support. Also two student
    tests are included to evaluate the students' factual knowledge as well as
    their analytical skills in relation to social action.

TABLE 10 ACTION LEARNING PROGRAMS FOR TEACHERS

Finding Community: A Guide to Community Research and Action	Teaching Guide to the Values Education Series
Preparer/Author: Ron Jones	Rodney F. Allen
Publisher: James E. Freel and Associates 577 College Avenue Palo Alto, CA 94306	McDougal, Littell and Company Box 1667-B Evanston, IL 60204
Date: 1971	1974
Grades: 9–12	7–12
Materials and Cost: Teacher's Guide ($ 3.45)	Teacher's Guide ($ 1.50)
Objectives: To help students explore how well existing institutions are serving the needs of people.	To serve as a useful resource for anyone interested in values education and to help teachers achieve social-self-realization.
Content: The guide describes a variety of issues and then offers procedures for local research. Issues include food costs, the welfare system, poverty, police and the school system.	The analysis, moral development, clarification and action learning approaches are all contained in the book.
Methods: Students first read about the social issues and the evidence about the issues from various primary sources. Then they determine through surveys and other procedures if the issues raised can also be found in their community. Other approaches to the issues are presented and students are then prepared to begin an actual project.	The primary method used is reading and this is supplemented with guidelines for evaluating students' growth in value education through videotape analysis, discussion, observations and self-analysis.
Critique: The premise of these materials is that students learn about their community by becoming involved in it.	This little book is an excellent resource and summary of values education materials, theory and supplemental readings and films.

Appendix G (Chapter 7)

CURRICULUM FLEXIBILITY CHECK LIST

═══════════════════════════════════

SCHOOL DISCIPLINE DESK BOOK

Curriculum Flexibility Check List

Date_____

I am a   ☐ Student   ☐ Teacher   ☐ Parent

This check list provides a way for you to express your opinions regarding possible ways we might modify our curriculum so that it is more responsive to student needs.

Prior to completing the check list you should be familiar with the material in Chapter 8 of the *School Discipline Desk Book*. One objective in modifying the curriculum is to improve student morale and thereby reduce discipline problems.

Please use an *X* to indicate the response which most nearly expresses your opinion. Please do not sign your name. Your responses are confidential.

	Strongly Agree	Agree	Disagree	Strongly Disagree
IN THIS SCHOOL:	1	2	3	4
1a. Our curriculum is well-defined and articulated.				
1b. We should do more than we are now doing to define and articulate the curriculum.				
2a. We now offer a variety of minicourses to our students.				
2b. We should do more than we are now doing to offer minicourses to our students.				
3a. Our school is now on the quarter system.				
3b. We should change our present calendar to a quarter system or similar system which will enable us to increase course offerings.				
4a. Our curriculum now includes a variety of outdoor education experiences.				
4b. We should do more than we are now doing to offer outdoor education experiences.				
5a. We are now offering a variety of Independent Study Programs.				
5b. We should do more than we are now doing to offer Independent Study Programs.				
6a. Individualized assignment sheets (contracts, LAP's, unipacs, etc.) are widely used.				
6b. Individualized assignment sheets should be more extensively used.				
7a. Several learning laboratories, for active learning opportunities, are available to our pupils.				
7b. More learning laboratories should be created.				
8a. A number of curriculum enrichment activities is offered to our students.				
8b. We should do more than we are doing now to offer curriculum enrichment activities.				
9a. Several seminars (small discussion classes) are now offered in our school.				
9b. We should do more than we are doing now to offer small discussion classes to our students.				
10a. A variety of alternative learning environments is available to our students.				
10b. We should do more than we are doing now to define and offer alternative learning environments to our students.				

	1	2	3	4

11a. We now offer a "Learning by Teaching" program.

11b. We should do more than we are doing now to offer "Learning by Teaching" programs.

12a. We now offer a values education program.

12b. We should do more than we are doing now to offer values education to our pupils.

13a.

13b·

Appendix H (Chapter 8)

BLAUVELT ELEMENTARY SCHOOL

Referral Form

Blauvelt Elementary School

South Orangetown Central School District

Cottage Lane

New York 10913

Dr. Jo Ann Shaheen, Principal

BLAUVELT ELEMENTARY SCHOOL

My Name is_____ Grade _____

I was sent to the office by _____

Today's date _____

I _____

_____

_____

Then, this happened:

The teacher had to spend her time with me while the rest of the children waited.

Some person was hurt.   Who _____

Some person was embarrassed.   Who _____

Some person began to cry.   Who _____

Something was broken or damaged.   What _____

Some of the other people in my class were not able to do their work.

The teacher was upset or angry because I didn't do what she asked me to do.

I wasted my time.

I lost.   What _____

I won.   What _____

Perhaps, it was none of these things listed above. Then, tell me, in your own words, what happened.

_____

_____

_____

Just before I did it, I was feeling:

alone	angry	beaten	bored
cheated	confused	cruel	defeated
disappointed in me	disappointed in other people		dumb
eager to impress the other children		embarrassed	happy
hateful	hopeless	hurt by unkind words	
ignored	inferior	jealous	left out
like crying	like a failure	lonely	overlooked
poor	proud of me	sad scared	shy
sorry for me	ugly	useless	wishy-washy

cut off from the other children or the teacher

or _____

I was feeling this way because _____

_____

_____

Instead of what I did, I might have:

told a child how I was feeling.	told the aide how I was feeling.
told the teacher how I was feeling.	asked the teacher for permission.
found some work to do that was interesting.	listened more carefully.
made a bargain with the teacher.	been more careful.

done nothing.   or _____

I could have _____

_____

_____

Since I chose to do what I did, I believe that the teacher, principal, or children should:

See that I repair the damage.	Spank me. Talk it over with me.
Tell my mother or father.	Tell me to pay for the damage and see that I do.
Apologize orally to me.	Who _____
Apologize in writing to me.	Who _____
Take away a privilege or a right.	What _____
Forget it and give me another chance.	Give me extra homework.
Help me. Praise me.	

_____

_____

Give your paper to Mrs. Russell.

Student is to meet with_____

Summary of decisions made in meeting: _____

_____

_____

_____

_____

_____

Note: Young children use a tape recording of this form so that they can fill it out even though they may have difficulty reading it.

Index